SHE

D0313223

THE AUSTRALIAN
Women's Weekly
party food

Substantial to stylish: impressive food to wow your guests

BAUER

MEDIA GROUP

CONTENTS

INTRODUCTION

Planning a party is lots of fun and a great way to bring people together. Finger food is a smart choice when entertaining, as small individual portions are easier to prepare and serve. Being the host of a party is all about being organised: the key to success is to plan ahead.

Where to start?

Well, obviously the first thing to do is to make a guest list, then choose the location and make sure it will fit the intended number of guests. No-one wants to be squashed together like sardines, even if they do like each other. Next, the time of day and the occasion will ultimately decide what recipes you choose for the menu. If the occasion is between mealtimes, light food can be served, whereas if it is at a time when a meal is usually served, the menu needs to be more substantial.

Choosing the menu

We've created a number of menus (see pages 6-7) to help guide you, along with advice on how much to serve; however there are limitless menus you can create using our delicious triple-tested recipes.

When creating the menu, start by choosing some classic recipes that you personally like and then mix them up with a few special dishes. If the occasion acts as a meal, feel free to choose items from both the 'light bites' and 'substantial' chapters of this book. The chapter titled 'little boxes', is full of recipes

that are ideal substitutes for a meal, and can easily be multiplied for greater quantities, as can most of these recipes.

The menu should be a balance of fresh and light flavours and heartier, more robust flavours. Include some vegetable-based dishes on your menu. As a rule of thumb, lighter flavours and tastes, which are often eaten cold, should be served first, progressing to more substantial dishes, which are often served hot.

We have included a mouth-watering chapter on 'sweet things' and, while

sweet finger food isn't essential, it makes for a memorable ending that your guests will appreciate.

Buying and preparing the food
A list and time plan will help keep you organised in the lead-up to the party. Once you've drawn up the menu, make a shopping list and divide it into fresh and dry goods, this way you can cross items off your list as you buy them. Having a list allows you to see exactly what has to be done and when. Some of the dishes can be prepared ahead of time,

while others need to be prepared on the day. A to-do plan is a great way to prevent any last minute panic, which means, as the host of the party, you can also have a good time.

Serving
Good presentation will make even the simplest of food look sensational. While you might not think you have much in the way of serving platters, utilise objects such as boards, baskets, bowls and glass jars. Line them with baking paper, brown paper,

white napkins or colourful fabrics to suit the occasion.

Provide guests with small napkins to wipe their hands while eating. If you are serving sticky items like chicken wings, pop a finger bowl or hand wipes on the table to help remove any sticky residue.

If the food needs to be passed around, bribe some friends or family to help with an offer of an early tasting. Alternatively, set up a buffet, or 'grazing table' as they are sometimes known, with food and encourage guests to help themselves.

MENUS

There are numerous factors to think about when deciding on how much food you'll need for a cocktail party. Consider the mix of your guests – men will eat more than women, as will teenagers. The longer the party and the larger the guest list, the more variety you'll need. As a rough guide for 12-20 guests for a 2-hour cocktail party, allow 6 varieties of finger food when the party is to act as a meal, and 6 pieces of food per person per hour. For more formal occasions, such as a wedding reception where no seated dinner is planned, allow 8-10 choices of food, with 3 pieces of food per person.

FORMAL COCKTAIL PARTY

This elegant selection of bites is perfect for a wedding or engagement party.

- lychee and raspberry fizz (pg 16)
- minted pea soup shots (pg 35)
- tuna tartare (pg 18)
- sushi squares (pg 22)
- tempura prawns with lime and chilli sauce (pg 79)
- chicken and almond finger sandwiches (pg 29)
- poached ocean trout salad with japanese dressing (pg 91)
- prosecco and raspberry jellies (pg 101)

COCKTAIL PARTY FOR A CROWD

For large groups it's important to have a menu with a mix of do-ahead items and those that can be done at the last minute.

- tea party tipple (pg 10)
- smoked salmon finger sandwiches (pg 28)
- chicken yakitori (pg 56)
- middle-eastern lamb sausage rolls (pg 55)
- chorizo, potato and herb frittata (pg 38)
- smoked ocean trout and pickled fennel buns (pg 64)
- cheesy risotto balls (pg 52)
- beef and bacon sliders (pg 70)
- trio of orange panna cottas (pg 110)

GIRL'S GET TOGETHER

Try this menu for a bridal or baby shower or an event where you need lighter, more delicate food, such as one in the middle of the day.

- scroppino with strawberry puree (pg 8)
- quail eggs with spiced salt (pg 59)
- roasted beetroot and red onion dip (pg 43)
- smoked salmon finger sandwiches (pg 28)
- cheesy risotto balls (pg 52)
- chicken and watercress pasta salad (pg 85)
- sumac strawberry meringue nests (pg 105)

BACKYARD BASH WITH THE BOYS

This menu is designed for big appetites – teenage parties, footy finals, even a buck's night.

- barbados (pg 13) (although not for teenagers!)
- crunchy salt and pepper prawns with sweet chilli syrup (pg 25)
- mustard dogs in pastry (pg 68)
- smoky barbecued pork ribs (pg 80)
- fried buttermilk and mustard chicken wings (pg 48)
- heirloom tomato and mozzarella salad (pg 87)
- paella with garlic aïoli (pg 95)
- black forest brownies with cherry chocolate ganache (pg 96)

FAMILY COCKTAIL PARTY

With lots of familiar favourites, this menu would suit any multi-generational family occasion.

- venice dusk (pg 13)
- five-spice squid with lime mayonnaise (pg 92)
- tomato, pancetta and buffalo mozzarella pizza (pg 76)
- chimichurri lamb cutlets (pg 73)
- sesame-crusted chicken goujons (pg 78)
- prawn pad thai (pg 82)
- strawberry toffee pops (pg 104)
- little portuguese custard tarts (pg 98)

SUMMER GARDEN PARTY

This summery menu is equally suited to a lunch or a balmy summer's night party.

- cucumber basil gimlet (pg 16)
- venice dusk (pg 13)
- fetta and black olive dip (pg 42)
- haloumi and avocado bruschetta (pg 26)
- korean barbecued squid on skewers (pg 67)
- moroccan lamb, mint and currant cigars (pg 20)
- sesame-crusted chicken goujons (pg 78)
- smoked ocean trout and pickled fennel buns (pg 64)
- elderflower and cranberry ice-pops (pg 101)

DRINKS

scroppino with strawberry puree

PREP TIME 15 MINUTES (+ REFRIGERATION) MAKES 12

375g (12 ounces) strawberries, chopped

¼ cup (60ml) elderflower cordial

⅓ cup (125ml) vodka, chilled

750ml (25 fluid-ounce) bottle prosecco
(Italian sparkling wine), chilled

3 litres (12 cups) lemon sorbet

1 Place glasses in the freezer to chill. Meanwhile, blend or process strawberries and cordial until smooth. Transfer to a jug; refrigerate until needed.
2 To make the scroppino: place half the vodka in a blender; slowly pour in half the wine, then add half the sorbet. Blend, in bursts, until combined.
3 Pour 1 tablespoon strawberry puree into the base of six chilled glass, top with scroppino; serve immediately. Repeat with remaining ingredients.

This traditional frozen Venetian drink made with gelato is hard to categorise – part drink, part dessert – with a texture more akin to a slushie. We've used sorbet instead of gelato but, either way, it's delicious; just be sure to serve it with long spoons or straws, if served in tall glasses.

tea party tipple

PREP TIME 15 MINUTES (+ REFRIGERATION) **MAKES** 5 CUPS

20cm stick (40g) fresh lemon grass

2 earl grey tea bags

⅓ cup (75g) caster (superfine) sugar

1½ cups (375ml) boiling water

1 medium lemon (140g), halved lengthways, sliced thinly

2 x 300ml bottles dry ginger ale, chilled

⅓ cup (80ml) strained lemon juice

1 cup (250ml) gin

ice-cubes, to serve

1 Trim lemon grass to 20cm (8-inches) long, cut in half lengthways; place in a heatproof jug. Add tea bags, sugar and the boiling water, stir until sugar dissolves; stand 10 minutes. Discard tea bags; cover, refrigerate until cold.

2 To serve, one-third fill a jug with ice; add lemon, tea mixture and lemon grass stalks. Stir in remaining ingredients with lemon grass stalks to combine.

tip For a decorative element, make your own tea bags with 4 small squares of muslin and ½ teaspoon loose tea in each; tie with string and leave in the jug to serve.

macchitino

PREP TIME 15 MINUTES (+ REFRIGERATION) **MAKES** 5 CUPS

2 green-tea tea bags

⅔ cup loosely packed fresh mint leaves

⅓ cup (75g) caster (superfine) sugar

2 cups (500ml) boiling water

1 medium green apple (150g), unpeeled, sliced thinly crossways

½ cup fresh mint sprigs

1 cup (250ml) gin, chilled

1⅓ cups (330ml) granny smith apple juice, chilled

2 tablespoons lime juice

ice-cubes, to serve

1 Place tea bags in a heatproof jug with mint and sugar. Pour over the boiling water, stir until sugar dissolves; stand 5 minutes. Strain through a fine sieve into a bowl, pressing down on solids to extract all liquid; discard solids. Refrigerate liquid, covered, until cold.

2 To serve, one-third fill a jug with ice, top with apple slices and mint; stir in tea, gin and apple and lime juices to combine. Pour into small glass tumblers or martini glasses.

test kitchen tip

Gin comes in differing styles, with juniper berry the principle flavour. Choose one with added botanicals (components derived from plants), which will give the cocktail a more rounded, complex taste.

venice dusk

venice dusk

PREP TIME 15 MINUTES (+ FREEZING) **MAKES** 8 CUPS

1kg (2-pound) piece seedless watermelon

6 wide strips mandarin rind

1 cup (250ml) vodka, chilled

¼ cup (55g) caster (superfine) sugar

1 cup (250ml) apéritif, chilled

3 cups (750ml) soda water, chilled

1 cup (250ml) strained mandarin juice

⅓ cup (80ml) strained lemon juice

ice-cubes, to serve

1 Cut rind from watermelon; cut flesh into 2cm (¾-inch) cubes, place in a ziptop bag; freeze 1 hour or until ready to use.

2 Half fill a jug with ice cubes, frozen watermelon and mandarin rind. Stir vodka and sugar in a small bowl until sugar dissolves; stir mixture into jug with remaining ingredients, serve immediately.

tip Apéritifs are made by infusing herbs and/or fruit in alcohol and water; they have a bitter taste and are characterised by their dark red colour. Use an apéritif such as Aperol or Campari.

barbados

PREP TIME 25 MINUTES **MAKES** 6 CUPS

8 passionfruit

1½ cups (330g) caster (superfine) sugar

1 cup (250ml) water

1 pineapple (1.2kg), peeled, halved, sliced thinly

4 medium oranges (960g)

1 cup (250ml) dark underproof rum, chilled

2 cups (500ml) lemonade, chilled

crushed ice, to serve

1 Remove pulp from passionfruit; reserve.
2 Place sugar in a large heavy-based frying pan over medium heat; cook, stirring until a dark caramel colour (the sugar will start to dissolve, then form clumps; as you continue to stir it will eventually liquefy).
3 Carefully add the water and passionfruit pulp to the sugar (the mixture will spit); when the bubbles subside, stir the mixture until smooth. Pour mixture into a large stainless steel bowl, add pineapple; turn to coat in mixture.
4 Cut 1 orange into slices; juice the remaining oranges. Add orange juice and slices to the bowl with the rum and lemonade; stir to combine.
5 One-third fill a jug with crushed ice. Add rum, mixture; serve immediately.

tip The caramel will burn if it touches your skin, so be extra careful when adding the liquid to the melted sugar. Add the liquid down the side of the pan, not over the top, keeping your arm well out of the way of the boiling caramel.

(photograph page 14)

test kitchen tip

Underproof rum has a
more mellow flavour,
which is just like life
in Barbados.

barbados (recipe page 13)

lychee and raspberry fizz (recipe page 16)

lychee and raspberry fizz

PREP TIME 15 MINUTES (+ FREEZING) **SERVES** 12

You need 2 x 12-hole ice-cube trays.

24 white sugar cubes (90g)

Angostura bitters

560g (1 pound) canned lychees in syrup

125g (4 ounces) frozen raspberries

1 cup (250ml) water, chilled

¼ cup (60ml) brandy

2 x 750ml (25 fluid-ounce) bottles prosecco (Italian sparkling wine), chilled

1 Place a sugar cube in each hole of the ice-cube trays; stain each cube with two drops of bitters.
2 Strain lychees over a bowl, reserve syrup; quarter lychees. Divide lychees and raspberries into ice-cube trays. Combine reserved lychee syrup and the water; pour into trays; freeze for 4 hours.
3 Unmould ice-cubes into a chilled bowl. To serve, place two ice-cubes into each cocktail glass, top with 1 teaspoon brandy; pour in wine. Serve immediately.

(photograph page 15)

cucumber basil gimlet

PREP TIME 15 MINUTES **MAKES** 5 CUPS

1¼ cups (275g) caster (superfine) sugar

1 cup firmly packed fresh basil leaves

5 lebanese cucumbers (650g), chopped coarsely

crushed ice

700ml gin, chilled

½ cup (125ml) strained lime juice

¼ cup fresh basil leaves, extra

1 lebanese cucumber, extra, sliced thinly lengthways

1 Process sugar, basil and chopped cucumber in a food processor until smooth.
2 Fill a large jug one-third full with crushed ice. Strain cucumber mixture through a fine sieve into jug, pushing down on solids to extract all liquid. Add gin and juice; stir well to combine. Top with extra basil and sliced cucumber to serve.

tip Use a vegetable peeler to thinly slice the cucumber lengthways.

cucumber basil gimlet

LIGHT BITES

tuna tartare

PREP + COOK TIME 30 MINUTES (+ COOLING) MAKES 36

You need 3 x 12-hole (1 tablespoon/20ml) mini muffin pans. If you only have one pan, that is fine, just cook the wonton cases in batches.

cooking-oil spray

36 square wonton wrappers

600g (1¼ pounds) sashimi-grade tuna, chopped finely

2 teaspoons finely grated lemon rind

2 tablespoons finely chopped cornichons

2 tablespoons finely chopped fresh flat-leaf parsley

2 tablespoons finely chopped fresh chives

2 tablespoons olive oil

3 shallots (75g), chopped finely

4 drained anchovy fillets, chopped finely

¼ cup (50g) rinsed, drained baby capers

2 tablespoons strained lemon juice

¼ cup trimmed fresh micro cress or finely chopped fresh parsley leaves or chives, extra, to serve

finely grated lemon rind, extra, to serve

1 Preheat oven to 180°C/350°F. Spray 3 x 12-hole (1 tablespoon/20ml) mini muffin pans with cooking oil. Press one wrapper into each pan hole; spray with cooking oil. Bake 7 minutes or until browned lightly and crisp. Cool on a wire rack.

2 Meanwhile, combine tuna, rind, cornichons, herbs, oil, shallots, anchovies and capers in a medium bowl. Season to taste.

3 Just before serving, stir juice into tuna mixture. Spoon mixture into wonton cups; top with cress and extra lemon rind, to serve.

do-ahead Wonton cups can be prepared a day ahead and stored in an airtight container.

test kitchen tip

You could also serve the tuna tartare in a bowl with a pile of home-cooked prawn crackers for guests to assemble themselves.

nutritional count per piece

▶ 1.4g total fat
▶ 0.2g saturated fat
▶ 215kJ (51 cal)
▶ 4.3g carbohydrate
▶ 23.8g protein
▶ 0.1g fibre

moroccan lamb, mint and currant cigars

PREP + COOK TIME 50 MINUTES (+ COOLING) **MAKES** 40

2 tablespoons olive oil

1 large brown onion (200g), chopped finely

2cm (¾-inch) piece fresh ginger (10g), grated finely

3 cloves garlic, crushed

2 tablespoons ras el hanout

500g (1 pound) minced (ground) lamb

1 medium tomato (150g), chopped finely

¼ cup (40g) dried currants

¼ cup coarsely chopped fresh mint

¼ cup coarsely chopped fresh coriander (cilantro)

¼ cup (40g) pine nuts, toasted

150g (4½ ounces) butter

20 sheets (440g) fillo pastry

1 teaspoon sumac

1½ cups (420g) greek-style yoghurt

1 Heat oil in a large frying pan. Add onion, ginger and garlic; cook, stirring, 2 minutes or until onion is softened. Add spice, stir 1 minute or until fragrant.
2 Add lamb, stir 5 minutes or until browned, breaking up lumps with a wooden spoon. Stir in tomato; season to taste. Cook a further 1 minute or until any liquid evaporates. Remove from heat; cool to room temperature. Add currants, herbs and nuts.
3 Meanwhile, preheat oven to 200°C/400°F.
4 Heat butter until just melted. Unroll fillo, place flat on a work surface; cover with a lightly dampened clean tea towel while you work to prevent it drying out. Working quickly, place one sheet of fillo on the work surface, brush with melted butter; cut in half crossways. Place 1 tablespoon of lamb mixture along base of fillo, leaving a 5cm (2-inch) border on each side.

5 Fold in sides of fillo to enclose filling; roll up tightly to form a cigar shape. Place 3cm (1¼-inches) apart on a baking-paper-lined oven tray. Repeat with remaining fillo, butter and filling.
6 Brush cigars with remaining butter; sprinkle with a little sumac. Bake 12 minutes or until browned and crisp. Serve with yoghurt.

do-ahead Filling can be made a day ahead; store, covered, in the fridge.

nutritional count per cigar
▶ 7.2g total fat
▶ 3.3g saturated fat
▶ 468kJ (112 cal)
▶ 7.2g carbohydrate
▶ 4.3g protein
▶ 0.5g fibre

sushi squares

PREP + COOK TIME 1 HOUR (+ REFRIGERATION & COOLING) **MAKES** 50

2 x 200g (6½ ounces) beef sirloin steaks

¼ cup (60ml) teriyaki marinade

3½ cups (875ml) water

2⅔ cups (530g) sushi rice

2 bunches thin asparagus (340g), trimmed

⅓ cup (100g) whole-egg or japanese mayonnaise

1 teaspoon wasabi paste

1 tablespoon finely chopped fresh chives

½ cup (125ml) sushi seasoning

2 nori sheets

2 tablespoons (30g) toasted sesame seeds

2 tablespoons (30g) black sesame seeds

soy sauce, for dipping

1 Grease a 20cm x 30cm (8-inch x 12-inch) slice pan, line with plastic wrap, extending 10cm (4-inches) above sides.

2 Combine beef with marinade in a medium bowl, cover; refrigerate 2 hours or overnight. Drain beef; discard marinade. Heat an oiled large frying pan over medium-high heat. Cook beef 2 minutes each side or until cooked as desired; remove from pan, cover loosely with foil, cool. Slice steaks thinly just before assembling.

3 Place the water and rice in a medium saucepan; bring to the boil. Reduce heat; simmer, covered, 12 minutes or until water is absorbed. Remove from heat; stand, covered 10 minutes.

4 Meanwhile, boil asparagus until just tender; refresh under cold water, drain on paper towel.

5 Combine mayonnaise, wasabi and chives in a medium bowl.

6 Transfer rice to a large, stainless steel or glass bowl. Gradually add sushi seasoning, stirring continuously with a spatula until combined. Cool completely, stirring occasionally.

7 To assemble sushi cake: using wet hands, press one-third of the rice mixture evenly into the base of the prepared pan; spread with half the mayonnaise mixture. Top with asparagus, then nori sheets, overlapping in centre. Spread another third of the rice mixture over nori, top with the remaining mayonnaise and the beef slices. Spread remaining rice mixture over beef; sprinkle half the combined sesame seeds over the top of the rice.

8 Cover sushi cake with a layer of plastic wrap. Carefully turn sushi cake out onto a chopping board similar in size to the pan. Carefully remove plastic wrap from top; sprinkle remaining sesame seeds over sushi cake. Replace plastic cover, turn sushi cake back into pan. Place a chopping board and a few heavy cans on top of the sushi cake; refrigerate for 1 hour.

9 Turn sushi cake out onto a chopping board; using a sharp, wet knife, cut into 4cm x 3cm (1½-inch x 1¼-inch) rectangles. Serve sushi with soy sauce.

do-ahead Sushi cake can be made 8 hours ahead; store in an airtight container in the refrigerator.

tips For variations on the filling, use a combination of smoked salmon (or crab meat or prawns) with cucumber, avocado and pickled vegetables. Sushi seasoning is a mixture of rice vinegar, sugar and salt; it is available in bottles from Asian food stores and the Asian food section of supermarkets.

nutritional count per square
▶ 2.9g total fat
▶ 0.5g saturated fat
▶ 358kJ (85 cal)
▶ 9.9g carbohydrate
▶ 4.5g protein
▶ 0.3g fibre

crunchy salt and pepper prawns with sweet chilli syrup

PREP + COOK TIME 45 MINUTES (+ STANDING) **MAKES** 30

30 uncooked medium prawns (shrimp) (800g)

¾ cup (55g) japanese breadcrumbs (panko)

1 teaspoon cracked black peppercorns

1½ teaspoons piri piri seasoning

2 teaspoons sea salt flakes

1 egg white, beaten lightly

vegetable oil, for deep-frying

1 fresh long red chilli, sliced thinly

2 tablespoons fresh coriander leaves (cilantro)

SWEET CHILLI SYRUP

½ cup (110g) white (granulated) sugar

½ cup (125ml) water

¼ cup (80g) sweet chilli sauce

4 kaffir lime leaves, torn

1cm (½-inch) piece fresh ginger (5g), sliced thinly

2 fresh coriander (cilantro) roots and stems, washed, sliced thinly

1 Make sweet chilli syrup.

2 Shell and devein prawns leaving tails intact.

3 Combine crumbs, pepper, seasoning and salt in a small bowl. Holding prawns by the tail, dip one at a time into egg white, then coat in crumb mixture.

4 Fill a large saucepan or deep-fryer one-third full with oil; heat to 180°C/350°F (or until a cube of bread turns golden in 10 seconds). Deep-fry prawns, in batches, for 1 minute or until cooked through and crisp. Drain on a paper towel.

5 Sprinkle prawns with chilli and coriander leaves; accompany with sweet chilli syrup for dipping.

SWEET CHILLI SYRUP Combine ingredients in a small saucepan; stir over medium heat until sugar dissolves. Bring to the boil; reduce heat, simmer, uncovered, about 5 minutes or until sauce thickens slightly. Remove from heat; stand 15 minutes, then discard lime leaves.

do-ahead The sauce can be made up to 2 days ahead; store, covered, in the fridge. Prawns can be crumbed 3 hours ahead; store, covered, in the fridge.

nutritional count per piece
▶ 0.9g total fat
▶ 0.1g saturated fat
▶ 188kJ (45 cal)
▶ 6.2g carbohydrate
▶ 3.1g protein
▶ 0.1g fibre

roast pumpkin and fetta bruschetta

PREP + COOK TIME 50 MINUTES **MAKES** 30

1 long french bread stick (300g)

cooking-oil spray

1.5kg (3-pound) butternut pumpkin

1 teaspoon dried chilli flakes

1½ teaspoons cumin seeds

2 tablespoons extra-virgin olive oil

½ cup (50g) walnuts, roasted, chopped coarsely

180g (5½ ounces) persian fetta, crumbled

1 tablespoon fresh thyme leaves

1 Preheat oven to 180°C/350°F. Line two oven trays with baking paper.
2 Trim rounded ends from bread. Cut bread into 30 x 1.5cm (¾-inch) thick slices; spray both sides with cooking oil. Place bread on oven trays. Bake 8 minutes or until browned lightly. Cool on trays.
3 Meanwhile, cut pumpkin lengthways into four slices about 3cm (1¼-inch) thick. Cut each piece into 5mm (¼-inch) thick slices.
4 Place pumpkin, spices and oil in a large bowl; toss well to combine. Arrange slices on two baking-paper-lined oven trays. Roast 25 minutes or until just tender.
5 Top bread with 3-4 pumpkin slices; sprinkle over walnuts, fetta and thyme. Drizzle with extra oil, if you like.

do-ahead Bread can be toasted 2 hours ahead; store in an airtight container. Pumpkin can be cooked 1 hour ahead.

nutritional count per piece
▶ 4.2g total fat
▶ 1.2g saturated fat
▶ 363kJ (86 cal)
▶ 8.9g carbohydrate
▶ 2.7g protein
▶ 1.5g fibre

haloumi and avocado bruschetta

PREP + COOK TIME 30 MINUTES (+ STANDING) **MAKES** 24

400g (12½-ounce) loaf afghan bread

cooking-oil spray

500g (1 pound) haloumi cheese

3 medium avocadoes (750g), chopped coarsely

1 medium red onion (170g), chopped finely

2 medium tomatoes (300g), chopped finely

1 tablespoon olive oil

2 tablespoons lemon juice

40g (1½ ounces) baby rocket leaves (arugula)

1 Preheat oven to 180°C/350°F. Line two oven trays with baking paper.
2 Trim rounded edges from bread to form a 16cm x 48cm (6½-inch x 19¼-inch) rectangle. Level top of bread; discard trimmings. Cut bread into 24 rectangles 4cm x 8cm long (1½-inch x 3¼-inch); spray both sides with cooking oil.
3 Place bread, cut-side up, on oven trays; bake 6 minutes or until browned lightly.
4 Cut haloumi into 24 thin slices; lay between 2 sheets of paper towel for 5 minutes.
5 Meanwhile, combine avocado, onion, tomato, oil and juice in a medium bowl. Season to taste.
6 Pan-fry haloumi, in batches, in an oiled large frying pan, for 1 minute each side or until browned.
7 Top bread with one slice of haloumi, some avocado mixture and a few rocket leaves to serve.

do-ahead Toast bread 2 hours ahead; store in an airtight container. Combine avocado mixture 1 hour ahead; store in the fridge. Haloumi is best cooked just before serving.

nutritional count per piece
▶ 11g total fat
▶ 4.3g saturated fat
▶ 720kJ (172 cal)
▶ 10.2g carbohydrate
▶ 7.3g protein
▶ 0.9g fibre

top: roast pumpkin and fetta bruschetta
bottom: haloumi and avocado bruschetta

smoked salmon finger sandwiches

PREP + COOK TIME 15 MINUTES MAKES 27

¾ cup (180g) crème fraîche

¼ cup finely chopped fresh chives

2 shallots (50g), chopped finely

18 large slices white bread (660g)

300g (9½ ounces) smoked salmon

1 Place crème fraîche, chives and shallots in a small bowl; stir to combine. Season to taste.
2 Spread half the bread slices with crème fraîche mixture; top with salmon, then sandwich with remaining bread.
3 Using a sharp serrated knife (or electric knife), trim crusts; cut each sandwich into three long fingers. (The trick to tidy-looking sandwiches is to use a fast sawing action, without applying pressure to cut the sandwiches.)
4 Cover sandwiches with lightly dampened paper towel, then plastic wrap; store in the fridge until ready to serve.

do-ahead Sandwiches can be made 3 hours ahead; store, covered, in the fridge. Bring to room temperature before serving.

nutritional count per piece
▶ 3.4g total fat
▶ 6.4g carbohydrate
▶ 1.8g saturated fat
▶ 4.1g protein
▶ 309kJ (73 cal)
▶ 0.5g fibre

chicken and almond sandwiches

PREP + COOK TIME 25 MINUTES MAKES 36

2½ cups (400g) finely chopped, boneless, skinless cooked chicken

½ cup (120g) sour cream

½ cup (150g) whole-egg mayonnaise

2 stalks celery (300g), trimmed, chopped finely

½ cup (40g) flaked almonds, toasted

50g (1½ ounces) baby rocket leaves (arugula), chopped coarsely

18 large slices wholegrain bread (810g)

1 Combine chicken, sour cream, mayonnaise, celery, nuts and rocket in large bowl. Season to taste.
2 Sandwich chicken mixture equally between bread slices.
3 Using a sharp serrated knife (or electric knife), trim crusts; cut sandwiches into quarters. (The trick to tidy-looking sandwiches is to use a fast sawing action, without applying pressure to cut the sandwiches).

do-ahead Chicken filling, without the nuts, can be made 3 hours ahead; store, covered, in the fridge; add the nuts just before assembling sandwiches to retain their crunch. Bring filling to room temperature before serving.

nutritional count per piece

▶ 6.1g total fat
▶ 1.4g saturated fat
▶ 409kJ (98 cal)
▶ 5.2g carbohydrate
▶ 5g protein
▶ 0.9g fibre

chicken skewers with green olives (recipe page 32)

chicken skewers with green olives (recipe page 32)

test kitchen tips

You will need 24 small bamboo skewers for this recipe; soak in cold water for 3 minutes before using to stop burning during cooking. Chicken thigh fillets are better to use than chicken breast meat as their higher fat content ensures the meat stays moist during barbecuing. Chicken can be marinated a day ahead; store, covered, in the fridge. You will need 2 lemons for this recipe.

chicken skewers with green olives

PREP + COOK TIME 30 MINUTES (+ REFRIGERATION)
MAKES 24

4 large chicken thigh fillets (800g)

3 cloves garlic, crushed

2 tablespoons finely chopped fresh oregano

2 teaspoons finely grated lemon rind

2 tablespoons strained lemon juice

2 tablespoons olive oil

lemon wedges, to serve

GREEN OLIVE DRESSING

½ cup (60g) pitted green olives

2 tablespoons fresh oregano leaves

⅓ cup (80ml) olive oil

1 Cut each thigh fillet into 6 long strips; combine with garlic, oregano, rind, juice and oil in a medium bowl; cover with plastic wrap, refrigerate 2 hours.
2 Make green olive dressing.
3 Thread one strip of chicken onto each skewer. Cook chicken, in batches, on a heated, oiled grill plate (or grill or barbecue) for 2 minutes each side or until cooked through.
4 Serve chicken skewers with dressing and wedges.

GREEN OLIVE DRESSING Coarsely chop 4 olives; reserve. Blend or process remaining ingredients until almost smooth. Transfer into serving bowl; top with chopped olives.

(photograph page 31)

---

nutritional count per skewer
▶ 9g total fat ▶ 5.2g carbohydrate
▶ 1.9g saturated fat ▶ 3.7g protein
▶ 487kJ (116 cal) ▶ 0.1g fibre

---

fish scrolls with capsicum salsa

PREP + COOK TIME 40 MINUTES **MAKES** 30

You need 30 small (15cm/6-inch) bamboo skewers, and a large banana leaf (see tips, right).

1kg (2-pound) piece firm white fish fillet, skin and bones removed

¼ cup (60ml) red wine vinegar

⅓ cup (80ml) olive oil

½ small red capsicum (bell pepper) (75g), chopped finely

½ small green capsicum (bell pepper) (75g), chopped finely

½ small red onion (50g), chopped finely

1 small tomato (90g), seeded, chopped finely

1 fresh long red chilli, seeded, sliced thinly

fresh coriander leaves (cilantro), to serve

1 Cut fish into 30 x 12cm (4¾-inch) strips, 1cm (½-inch) thick; roll each strip into a scroll, secure with a skewer; season.
2 Combine vinegar and oil in a small saucepan; stir over low heat for 3 minutes or until warm – do not boil. Combine capsicum, onion and tomato in a small bowl; pour over warmed vinegar mixture, season to taste.
3 Meanwhile, heat an oiled large frying pan over medium-high heat; pan-fry fish, in batches, for 1½ minutes each side or until just cooked through.
4 Cut banana leaves into large rectangles; serve fish on banana leaves with capsicum salsa.

---

nutritional count per scroll
▶ 3.9g total fat ▶ 0.2g carbohydrate
▶ 0.7g saturated fat ▶ 6.8g protein
▶ 268kJ (64 cal) ▶ 0.1g fibre

Banana leaves can be ordered from fruit and vegetable stores. Cut with a sharp knife close to the main stem, then immerse in hot water so the leaves will be pliable. Depending on the shape of the fish, you may need to roll two pieces of fish together.

fish scrolls with capsicum salsa

cauliflower, dill and cumin fritters

cauliflower, dill and cumin fritters

PREP + COOK TIME 30 MINUTES
MAKES 40

1 cup (150g) self-raising flour

¼ cup (35g) chickpea (besan) flour

½ teaspoon cayenne pepper

2 tablespoons ground cumin

2 teaspoons salt

⅓ cup coarsely chopped fresh dill

1 egg, beaten lightly

1⅓ cups (330ml) chilled water

700g (1½ pounds) cauliflower

vegetable oil, for deep-frying

1 Combine flours, spices, salt and dill in a medium bowl. Make a well in the centre; add the egg and enough water to make a smooth batter. Cover, stand 10 minutes.
2 Meanwhile, trim cauliflower into large florets; cut florets into 1cm (½-inch) thick slices (you will have approximately 40 pieces).
3 Fill a large saucepan or deep fryer one-third full with oil; heat to 180°C/350°F (or until a cube of bread turns golden in 10 seconds). Dip cauliflower, piece by piece, in batter, shaking off excess. Fry, in batches, for 2 minutes, turning halfway through cooking, or until golden in colour. Drain fritters on paper towel.

do-ahead Florets can be cut 3 hours ahead.
tip Accompany with greek-style yoghurt mixed with a pinch of cayenne pepper, if you like.

---

minted pea soup shots

PREP + COOK TIME 35 MINUTES
MAKES 2 LITRES SERVES 24

30g (1 ounce) butter

1 medium leek (350g), white part only, chopped finely

1 clove garlic, crushed

1 medium potato (200g), chopped finely

1 litre (4 cups) chicken stock

½ cup (125ml) pouring cream

1kg (2 pounds) frozen baby peas

¼ cup finely shredded fresh mint

½ cup (120g) light sour cream

freshly cracked pepper

1 Heat butter in a large saucepan over medium heat. Add leek, garlic and potato; cook, stirring, 3 minutes or until leek softens.
2 Add stock and cream, bring to the boil; reduce heat, simmer, covered, for 5 minutes or until potato is tender. Add peas and mint, simmer, 10 minutes. Season to taste, cool 10 minutes.
3 Blend or process soup mixture until smooth, thinning with a little water if soup is too thick. Pour among ⅓-cup heatproof glasses, cups or shot glasses. To serve, drop teaspoons of sour cream onto soup, sprinkle with pepper.

do-ahead Soup can be made a day ahead; reheat just before serving, then finish with sour cream and pepper. Sprinkle soup with micro mint leaves to serve, if you like.

(photograph page 36)

---

nutritional count per fritter
▶ 2g total fat   ▶ 3.7g carbohydrate
▶ 0.3g saturated fat   ▶ 1.9g protein
▶ 162kJ (38 cal)   ▶ 0.6g fibre

nutritional count per serving
▶ 4.2g total fat   ▶ 4.3g carbohydrate
▶ 2.6g saturated fat   ▶ 3.2g protein
▶ 314kJ (75 cal)   ▶ 3.5g fibre

minted pea soup shots (recipe page 35)

chorizo, potato and herb frittata

PREP + COOK TIME 1¼ HOURS **MAKES** 45

5 large potatoes (1.5kg), unpeeled

1 tablespoon olive oil

4 cured chorizo sausages (450g), sliced thinly

1 large brown onion (200g), sliced thinly

50g baby rocket leaves (arugula), chopped coarsely

½ cup coarsely chopped fresh flat-leaf parsley

1 cup (120g) grated cheddar

12 eggs

300ml pouring cream

lemon wedges and extra rocket, to serve

1 Boil, steam or microwave potatoes until just tender. When cool enough to handle, peel skins, then cut flesh into 1cm (½-inch) cubes.

2 Preheat oven to 160°C/325°F. Grease a deep 24cm x 35cm (9½-inch x 13¾-inch) baking pan; line base and sides with baking paper, extending paper 7cm (2¾-inches) above sides.

3 Meanwhile, heat oil in a large frying pan over medium heat. Add chorizo and onion; cook, stirring, for 5 minutes or until chorizo is browned. Cool 10 minutes.

4 Combine potatoes, half the chorizo mixture, rocket, parsley and cheese in baking pan.

5 Whisk eggs and cream together in a medium bowl; season to taste. Pour over potato mixture; top with remaining chorizo mixture. Bake, in oven, 35 minutes or until set. (To check, insert a skewer; no wet egg mixture should be visible.) Cool in pan.

6 Turn frittata onto a chopping board; trim edges. Cut into 3.5cm x 4.5cm (1½-inch x 1¾-inch) pieces. Turn pieces right-way up to serve. Serve topped with extra rocket and accompany with wedges.

do-ahead Frittata can be made a day ahead, store, covered, in the fridge; cut when ready to serve. To reheat, place frittata pieces close together on a baking-paper-lined oven tray in a preheated 160°C/325°F oven, for 25 minutes or until heated through.

nutritional count per piece
▶ 7.1g total fat
▶ 3.5g saturated fat
▶ 437kJ (104 cal)
▶ 4.2g carbohydrate
▶ 5.5g protein
▶ 0.6g fibre

test kitchen tip

Buy fresh, thin-style pitta bread; if the bread is too thick it may not sit well in the patty pan.

middle-eastern salad cups

PREP + COOK TIME 40 MINUTES (+ COOLING) **MAKES** 28

You need 3 x 12-hole (2-tablespoon/40ml) deep flat-based patty pans; it's fine if you only have one pan, just make the cups in batches. You also need an 8cm (3¼-inch) round cutter.

1 large potato (300g), unpeeled

2 x 26cm (10½-inch) round pitta breads

¼ cup (60ml) olive oil

2 medium lebanese cucumbers (340g)

2 large tomatoes (440g), seeded, chopped finely

½ small red onion (50g), chopped finely

2 small red radishes (70g), trimmed, sliced thinly

2 tablespoons finely chopped fresh mint

¼ cup finely chopped fresh flat-leaf parsley

extra sumac and small fresh flat-leaf parsley sprigs, to serve

SUMAC DRESSING

1 clove garlic, crushed

1 teaspoon sumac

1 teaspoon sea salt flakes

¼ cup (60ml) lemon juice

¼ cup (60ml) olive oil

nutritional count per cup
▶ 4.3g total fat
▶ 0.7g saturated fat
▶ 231kJ (55 cal)
▶ 3g carbohydrate
▶ 0.7g protein
▶ 0.6g fibre

1 Preheat oven to 200°C/400°F. Oil 3 x 12-hole (2-tablespoon/40ml) deep flat-based patty pans.
2 Boil, steam or microwave potato until just tender. When cool enough to handle, peel, chop finely; cool.
3 Meanwhile, place a piece of bread on a work surface. Using the 8cm round cutter, cut out seven bread rounds; separate rounds into two layers. Repeat with remaining bread; you will have 28 bread rounds. Brush inside (rough side) of each round with a little of the oil.
4 Firmly push bread rounds, oiled-side up, into pan holes. Bake for 5 minutes or until golden; cool.
5 Meanwhile, make sumac dressing.
6 Seed and finely chop one cucumber. Combine potato, chopped cucumber, tomato and onion in a medium bowl. Add dressing, stir gently to combine.
7 To serve, using a vegetable peeler, cut remaining cucumber into thin slices; place into each bread cup with a few slices of radish. Spoon 1 tablespoon salad into each bread cup; sprinkle with extra sumac and mint, top with a parsley sprig.

SUMAC DRESSING Combine ingredients in a small screw-top jar; shake well to combine.

do-ahead Bread cups can be made a day ahead; store in an airtight container.

fetta and black olive dip

PREP TIME 10 MINUTES MAKES 5 CUPS

1 cup (150g) pitted black olives, chopped coarsely

2 tablespoons coarsely chopped fresh
flat-leaf parsley

400g (14 ounces) greek fetta, crumbled

250g (8 ounces) spreadable cream cheese

1½ cups (420g) greek-style yoghurt

1 teaspoon dried mint

fresh flat-leaf parsley sprigs, to serve

toasted pitta, crackers, grissini sticks or crudités,
to serve

1 Reserve ¼ cup of the olives.
2 Process remaining ingredients in a food processor
until smooth. Season with pepper. (You will not need
salt as both the olives and fetta are already salty.)
3 Spoon dip into a bowl, scatter with reserved
olives and parsley to serve. Drizzle with olive oil,
if you like.

tip Use greek fetta for taste and texture. Use
Kalamata olives, if you like.

---

nutritional count per 1 tablespoon

▶ 3.9g total fat   ▶ 1g carbohydrate

▶ 2.4g saturated fat   ▶ 1.8g protein

▶ 198kJ (47 cal)   ▶ 0g fibre

roasted beetroot and red onion dip

PREP + COOK TIME 2 HOURS (+ COOLING) MAKES 5 CUPS

5 medium beetroot (800g), trimmed

1 medium bulb garlic (70g)

2 medium red onions (340g), quartered

1 tablespoon fresh thyme leaves

cooking-oil spray

1½ cups (360g) sour cream

1 cup (100g) walnuts, toasted

1 tablespoon red wine vinegar

pan-fried pitta, turkish bread fingers, crackers or crudités, to serve

1 Preheat oven to 180°C/350°F. Line oven tray with baking paper.

2 Place beetroot, garlic, onion and thyme on an oven tray. Spray with cooking oil; season. Bake for 1 hour. Remove garlic, onion and thyme from tray. Cover beetroot with foil; bake a further 45 minutes or until tender. When cool enough to handle, remove and discard skins. Chop beetroot coarsely.

3 Squeeze garlic cloves from bulb. Blend or process beetroot with garlic, onion, thyme, sour cream, nuts and vinegar until smooth. Season to taste.

do-ahead Dip can be prepared a day ahead; store, covered, in the fridge.

nutritional count per 1 tablespoon

▶ 3.9g total fat   ▶ 1.7g carbohydrate

▶ 1.7g saturated fat   ▶ 0.8g protein

▶ 196kJ (46 cal)   ▶ 0.7g fibre

dukkah-crusted lamb with smoked eggplant dip

PREP + COOK TIME 40 MINUTES (+ REFRIGERATION & STANDING) MAKES 12

1 tablespoon olive oil

2 tablespoons dukkah

600g (1¼ pounds) lamb backstraps

extra olive oil and fresh flat-leaf parsley, to serve

EGGPLANT DIP

1 large eggplant (500g)

1 clove garlic, crushed

1 teaspoon sea salt flakes

1 teaspoon ground cumin

1 tablespoon finely chopped fresh flat-leaf parsley

2 tablespoons tahini

¼ cup (60ml) lemon juice

1 Combine oil, dukkah and lamb in a medium bowl; cover, refrigerate 2 hours.

2 Meanwhile, make eggplant dip.

3 Stand lamb at room temperature for 15 minutes. Heat an oiled grill plate or frying pan over medium heat. Cook lamb for 3 minutes each side (for medium rare) or until cooked as desired. Cover lamb; rest for 5 minutes before slicing thinly, season.

4 Top 1 tablespoon of dip with 3 slices of lamb; drizzle with extra oil and sprinkle with torn fresh flat-leaf parsley, if you like.

EGGPLANT DIP Prick eggplant all over with a fork. Grill over medium heat on an oiled grill plate for 25 minutes, turning frequently, or until tender. When cool enough to handle, peel eggplant. Squeeze eggplant flesh to remove any excess juice. Blend or process eggplant with remaining ingredients until smooth. Season to taste.

tips You will need 36 small decorative bamboo forks or skewers to serve. You can barbecue the lamb, instead of grilling or pan-frying, if you like.
do-ahead The eggplant dip can be made a day ahead; store, covered, in the fridge. The lamb can be marinated a day ahead; store, covered, in the fridge.

nutritional count per piece
▶ 7.4g total fat
▶ 1.6g saturated fat
▶ 517kJ (123 cal)
▶ 1.3g carbohydrate
▶ 12.3g protein
▶ 1.4g fibre

test kitchen tips

Dukkah is a packaged spice
and nut blend; it is available
from spice shops, major
supermarkets and delis.

gravlax

PREP + COOK TIME 30 MINUTES (+ REFRIGERATION) **SERVES** 12

½ cup (150g) rock salt

½ cup (110g) white (granulated) sugar

⅔ cup coarsely chopped fresh dill

2 teaspoons finely grated lime rind

2 teaspoons white peppercorns, crushed

1 tablespoon juniper berries, crushed

⅓ cup (80ml) gin

750g (1½-pound) centre-cut piece salmon fillet, skin-on, bones removed

2 tablespoons lime juice

2 tablespoons olive oil

crème fraîche and toasted french bread stick, pumpernickel bread or crackers, to serve

HERB SALAD

2 punnets micro herbs, trimmed

¼ cup fresh dill sprigs

1 Combine salt, sugar, dill, rind, pepper, berries and gin in a medium bowl. Spread half the gin mixture over the base of a shallow 20cm x 28cm (8-inch x 11¼-inch) ceramic or glass dish. Place salmon, skin-side down, over mixture. Top with remaining gin mixture.

2 Cover with plastic wrap. Place another dish on top, weigh down with cans of food. Refrigerate 24-36 hours, turning salmon every 12 hours.

3 Remove salmon from dish; scraping away any loose mixture, discard gin mixture. Pat salmon dry with paper towel.

4 Holding a knife at a 45 degree angle, and using long strokes, slice salmon across the grain as thinly as possible. Arrange slices on a large platter.

5 Just before serving, make herb salad. Drizzle salmon with juice and oil; top with herb salad. Serve with crème fraîche and crackers, if you like.

HERB SALAD Combine herbs in a small bowl.

tip Juniper berries can be found in good delis, spice shops and greengrocers.

nutritional count per serving
▶ 10.9g total fat
▶ 2.5g saturated fat
▶ 744kJ (177 cal)
▶ 1.4g carbohydrate
▶ 17.8g protein
▶ 0g fibre

test kitchen tips

You could substitute vodka for gin or omit the alcohol completely. Micro herbs are small punnets of various baby herbs or cress available at good greengrocers or growers' markets. Alternatively, use the smallest torn leaves from a regular bunch of herbs.

SUBSTANTIAL

fried buttermilk and mustard chicken wings

PREP + COOK TIME 40 MINUTES (+ REFRIGERATION) SERVES 12

1 cup (300g) rock salt

1 cup (220g) firmly packed brown sugar

2 tablespoons finely grated lemon rind

2 tablespoons finely chopped fresh lemon thyme

1 clove garlic, crushed

1.5kg (3 pounds) chicken wing nibbles

¾ cup (105g) plain (all-purpose) flour, plus extra, to dust

600ml (1 pint) buttermilk

2 tablespoons hot english mustard

1 egg, beaten lightly

vegetable oil, to deep-fry

1 Place salt, sugar, rind, thyme and garlic in a large bowl; mix to combine. Add chicken, toss well to coat; cover, refrigerate 1 hour.

2 Wash salt mixture from chicken under cold water; pat chicken dry with paper towel.

3 Place flour in a large bowl; gradually whisk in combined buttermilk, mustard and egg. Season.

4 Fill a large saucepan or deep fryer one-third full with oil; heat over medium heat to 180°C/350°F (or until a cube of bread turns golden in 10 seconds). Working in batches, dust chicken in extra flour. Dip chicken into batter; drain excess batter. Deep fry chicken, in batches, turning halfway through cooking time, for 6 minutes or until golden and cooked through. Remove with a slotted spoon; drain on paper towel.

5 Place chicken on a large platter to serve.

tips Sprinkle with lemon salt to serve, if you like: Combine ½ cup sea salt flakes, the thinly sliced rind of 2 lemons and 2 tablespoons finely chopped fresh lemon thyme in a small bowl.
Chicken wing nibbles are available from most major supermarkets. You could also use chicken drumettes.

nutritional count per serving
▸ 15.6g total fat
▸ 3.7g saturated fat
▸ 1055kJ (252 cal)
▸ 12.1g carbohydrate
▸ 16g protein
▸ 0.2g fibre

mediterranean lamb meatballs

PREP + COOK TIME 40 MINUTES MAKES 60

1kg (2 pounds) minced (ground) lamb

1½ cups (105g) stale breadcrumbs

1 large red onion (300g), chopped finely

2 tablespoons finely chopped fresh chervil

2 tablespoons finely chopped fresh
flat-leaf parsley

2 tablespoons finely chopped fresh mint

2 teaspoons caraway seeds, toasted

1 teaspoon ground cumin

1 teaspoon ground cinnamon

½ teaspoon ground cloves

2 eggs, beaten lightly

¼ cup (60ml) iced water

vegetable oil, for shallow-frying

WHITE BEAN DIP

400g (13 ounces) canned white beans,
rinsed, drained

1 clove garlic, crushed

2 tablespoons extra virgin olive oil

1 tablespoon tahini

2 teaspoons finely grated lemon rind

2 tablespoons lemon juice

1 tablespoon coarsely chopped fresh
flat-leaf parsley

test kitchen tips

Alternatively, cook meatballs over high heat on a lightly oiled barbecue grill plate, turning frequently, for 7 minutes, or until browned and cooked through.

1 To make meatballs, place all ingredients in a large bowl, season; mix well to combine. Using damp hands, roll tablespoons of lamb mixture into balls.

2 Fill a large frying pan with 1cm (½-inch) oil; heat over medium heat. Shallow-fry meatballs, in 4 batches, turning frequently, for 5 minutes or until browned and cooked through. (You will need to replenish the oil slightly with each batch.) Remove with tongs or a slotted spoon; drain on paper towel.

3 Meanwhile, make white bean dip. Serve meatballs on a platter; accompany with dip.

WHITE BEAN DIP Process ingredients until smooth.

do-ahead Meatballs can be shaped a day ahead; store, covered, in the fridge.

nutritional count per piece
▶ 6.1g total fat
▶ 1.4g saturated fat
▶ 337kJ (80 cal)
▶ 1.9g carbohydrate
▶ 4.5g protein
▶ 0.5g fibre

cheesy risotto balls

PREP + COOK TIME 1¼ HOURS (+ COOLING) **MAKES** ABOUT 50

40g (1½ ounces) butter

1 medium brown onion (150g), chopped finely

2 cloves garlic, crushed

2 cups (400g) arborio rice

½ cup (125ml) dry white wine

1 litre (4 cups) hot chicken stock

½ cup (125ml) pouring cream

½ cup (50g) grated mozzarella

1 cup (80g) grated parmesan

2 egg yolks

1½ cups (110g) japanese breadcrumbs (panko)

vegetable oil, for deep-frying

1 Heat butter in a medium saucepan over medium heat, add onion and garlic; cook, stirring, 2 minutes or until onion is softened. Add rice, stir to coat rice in mixture.

2 Add wine to pan; cook, stirring, 2 minutes or until wine has evaporated. Gradually add hot stock, 1 cup at a time, stirring continuously, for 25 minutes or until all stock is used and the rice is just cooked. Add cream; cook, stirring, a further 2 minutes.

3 Remove from heat, stir in both cheeses. Cool 20 minutes, then add egg yolks; season. Spread rice over a baking-paper-lined oven tray; cool 15 minutes or until cool enough to handle.

4 Divide risotto into slightly rounded tablespoons of mixture. With wet hands, roll rice mixture into balls, then into breadcrumbs to coat.

5 Fill a large saucepan or deep fryer one-third full with oil; heat to 180°C/350°F (or until a cube of bread turns golden in 10 seconds). Fry risotto balls, in batches, for 2 minutes, stirring occasionally, or until browned and heated through. Drain on paper towel. Cool 5 minutes before serving.

do-ahead Risotto mixture can be made and rolled into balls a day ahead; store, covered, in the fridge. Roll in crumbs just before frying.

nutritional count per piece
▶ 5g total fat
▶ 1.9g saturated fat
▶ 362kJ (86 cal)
▶ 8.1g carbohydrate
▶ 2g protein
▶ 0.1g fibre

test kitchen tips

Middle-Eastern spice blend is available from supermarkets. Substitute with 1 tablespoon each cumin and coriander mixed with ½ teaspoon each turmeric and cardamom. Serve with greek-style yoghurt, tomato chutney or tomato sauce (ketchup) flavoured with a little pomegranate molasses and a pinch of ground allspice.

middle-eastern sausage rolls

PREP + COOK TIME 45 MINUTES (+ REFRIGERATION) **MAKES** 32

4 shallots (100g), chopped finely

3 cloves garlic, crushed

1kg (2 pounds) minced (ground) lamb

2 tablespoons tomato paste

½ cup (50g) packaged breadcrumbs

½ cup (70g) pistachios, chopped coarsely

¼ cup finely chopped fresh coriander (cilantro)

¼ cup (32g) middle-eastern spice blend

3 teaspoons fennel seeds

3 eggs

4 sheets puff pastry

sea salt flakes, for sprinkling

1 Place shallot, garlic, lamb, paste, breadcrumbs, pistachios, coriander, spice blend, 1 teaspoon of the fennel seeds and 2 eggs in a large bowl, season; mix well to combine. Cover; refrigerate for 3 hours to allow flavours to develop.
2 Preheat oven to 200°C/400°F. Line oven trays with baking paper.
3 Beat remaining egg lightly. Fill a large piping bag with lamb mixture. Cut pastry in half; pipe lamb mixture 4cm (1½-inches) wide, down one long edge of the pastry. Brush the opposite long edge with beaten egg; roll tightly to enclose. Repeat with remaining pastry, lamb mixture and egg.
4 Score pastry at ½cm (⅛-inch) intervals. Brush rolls with beaten egg; cut each roll into four pieces, sprinkle with remaining fennel seeds and the salt.
5 Place rolls, seam-side down, on oven trays; bake 25 minutes or until golden and cooked through. Serve immediately.

do-ahead Sausage rolls can be made and frozen in advance. Allow an extra 10 minutes when baking from frozen.

nutritional count per roll
- 11.7g total fat
- 5.2g saturated fat
- 799kJ (190 cal)
- 11.4g carbohydrate
- 9.6g protein
- 0.7g fibre

chicken yakitori

PREP + COOK TIME 30 MINUTES (+ REFRIGERATION) **MAKES** 24

You need 24 x 15cm (6-inch) bamboo skewers.

2 tablespoons jasmine rice

⅓ cup (80ml) tamari or soy sauce

¼ cup (60ml) sake

¼ cup (60ml) mirin

½ cup (110g) caster (superfine) sugar

2 teaspoons chinese five spice

2 tablespoons finely grated orange rind

2 tablespoons grape-seed oil

24 chicken tenderloins (1.2kg)

2 green onions (scallions), sliced thinly on the diagonal

1 Heat a medium frying pan over medium heat. Add rice; toast, stirring frequently, for 5 minutes or until fragrant and light golden. Transfer to a mortar and pestle; pound until finely ground.

2 Place tamari, sake, mirin, sugar and spice in a small saucepan over medium heat. Bring to a simmer; cook 2 minutes or until sugar dissolves. Remove from heat, add rind and oil. Transfer to a small bowl; refrigerate marinade until cool.

3 Combine tenderloins with marinade; refrigerate 3 hours or overnight.

4 Preheat a barbecue or grill pan over high heat. Drain chicken tenderloins from marinade; reserve marinade in a small bowl. Thread one tenderloin onto each skewer in a 'S' shape. Cook skewers, brushing with reserved marinade, for 8 minutes, turning frequently, until charred and chicken is cooked through.

5 To serve, place skewers on a platter, sprinkle over toasted rice and green onions.

tip Soak bamboo skewers for at least 30 minutes before using, to prevent burning when cooking.
do-ahead Chicken can be skewered and marinated a day ahead.

nutritional count per skewer
▶ 2.3g total fat
▶ 0.4g saturated fat
▶ 407kJ (97 cal)
▶ 7.1g carbohydrate
▶ 11.5g protein
▶ 0g fibre

za'atar pizza

PREP + COOK TIME 15 MINUTES **MAKES** 24 PIECES

430g (14-ounce) loaf turkish bread

2 tablespoons extra-virgin olive oil

2 tablespoons fresh flat-leaf parsley leaves

1½ cups (420g) greek-style yoghurt

ZA'ATAR MIXTURE

½ teaspoon sumac

¼ teaspoon salt

2 tablespoons za'atar

¼ cup olive oil

1 Preheat oven to 240°C/475°F.

2 Combine ingredients for za'atar mixture in a small bowl.

3 Cut bread in half horizontally. Spread za'atar mixture over cut halves. Place bread on oven tray; bake for 7 minutes.

4 Drizzle pizza with oil; cut into 12 triangles. Sprinkle with parsley; accompany with yoghurt.

tip The turkish bread should be about 13cm x 46cm (5¼-inches x 18½-inches) long. Za'atar is a mix of sumac, sesame seeds, salt and thyme. It is available from Middle-Eastern delis and major supermarkets.

do-ahead Make pizza 4 hours ahead; reheat in a slow (150°C/300°F) oven.

nutritional count per piece
- ▶ 6g total fat
- ▶ 1.5g saturated fat
- ▶ 458kJ (109 cal)
- ▶ 10.9g carbohydrate
- ▶ 2.6g protein
- ▶ 0.5g fibre

57

quail eggs with spiced salt

quail eggs with spiced salt

PREP + COOK TIME 15 MINUTES **MAKES** 24

1½ teaspoons celery seeds

1 teaspoon cumin seeds

1 teaspoon fennel seeds

½ teaspoon sumac

3 teaspoons brown sugar

1 teaspoon sea salt flakes

24 quail eggs

1 Place celery, cumin and fennel seeds in a saucepan over medium heat. Cook, stirring frequently, 2 minutes or until fragrant. Using a mortar and pestle, grind seed mixture to a powder. Cool completely; stir in sumac, sugar and salt.

2 Place eggs in a medium saucepan of boiling water; cook 2½ minutes for soft-boiled eggs or 3 minutes for hard-boiled. Drain; refresh in iced water. For easier peeling, peel eggs while still slightly warm.

3 Scatter salt mixture evenly over a tray, then roll quail eggs in salt.

4 To serve, place eggs on chinese soup spoons or mismatched teaspoons on a platter.

tip Quail eggs are available from selected butchers and delicatessens. Alternatively, place an order with your local butcher a few days in advance. We scattered trimmed baby lamb's lettuce over the eggs to serve.

nutritional count per egg

▶ 1.1g total fat ▶ 0.6g carbohydrate
▶ 0g saturated fat ▶ 1.1g protein
▶ 72kJ (17 cal) ▶ 1g fibre

polenta, blue cheese and fig tarts

PREP + COOK TIME 20 MINUTES **MAKES** 24

2 cups (500ml) milk

½ cup (80g) instant polenta

½ cup (40g) finely grated parmesan

2 tablespoons finely chopped fresh chives

24 x 6cm (2½-inch) small tart cases (220g)

12 small fresh figs (600g), halved lengthways

150g (5 ounces) blue cheese, crumbled

½ cup loosely packed fresh chervil sprigs

¼ cup (60ml) balsamic glaze

1 To make polenta, place milk in a small, heavy-based saucepan over medium heat; bring to a simmer. Whisking continuously, gradually add polenta in a thin stream; whisk for 5 minutes or until cooked and thickened. Remove from heat; stir in parmesan and chives. Season to taste.

2 Place about 1 tablespoon of polenta into each tart shell. Top with fig halves; sprinkle over blue cheese. (If the polenta thickens too much on standing, thin it by gradually whisking in a little extra milk, see tips page 60.)

3 Place tarts on a large platter; top with chervil sprigs, drizzle with balsamic glaze.

(photograph page 60)

nutritional count per tart

▶ 5.6g total fat ▶ 11.7g carbohydrate
▶ 3.3g saturated fat ▶ 3.9g protein
▶ 486kJ (116 cal) ▶ 0.8g fibre

test kitchen tips

Instant polenta, available from supermarkets, comes with cooking times varying from 1-5 minutes, so it's always best to read the packet directions. To keep polenta warm when serving, place polenta in a heatproof bowl placed over a saucepan of simmering water. Stir occasionally to prevent a skin from forming.
If fresh figs are out of season, substitute with dried figs.

polenta, blue cheese and fig tarts (recipe page 59)

test kitchen tip

Use a good-quality beef stock, as it will make all the difference to the flavour of these pies. It can be found frozen at delis and butchers.

nutritional count per pie

▶ 12.3g total fat
▶ 5.7g saturated fat
▶ 898kJ (215 cal)
▶ 16g carbohydrate
▶ 8.9g protein
▶ 0.7g fibre

red wine and rosemary mini beef pies

PREP + COOK TIME 50 MINUTES (+ REFRIGERATION) **MAKES** 24

You need 2 x 12-hole (⅓-cup/80ml) muffin pans, and both a 9cm (3¾-inch) and 6cm (2½-inch) round cutter.

2 tablespoons olive oil

1 large onion (200g), sliced thinly

2 cloves garlic, crushed

600g (1¼ pounds) minced (ground) beef

2 tablespoons finely chopped fresh rosemary

1 tablespoon finely chopped fresh lemon thyme

1 tablespoon finely chopped fresh flat-leaf parsley

2 tablespoons tomato paste

¾ cup (180ml) red wine

1½ tablespoons HP sauce

1 cup (250ml) beef stock

2 teaspoons cornflour (cornstarch)

3 sheets shortcrust pastry

2 sheets puff pastry

1 egg, beaten lightly

24 small fresh rosemary sprigs

1 Heat oil in a large saucepan over high heat. Add onion and garlic; cook, stirring, for 5 minutes or until onion is soft. Add beef and chopped herbs; cook, stirring, breaking beef up with a spoon, for 8 minutes or until browned. Stir in paste, red wine and sauce. Cook, stirring occasionally, 3 minutes or until wine has reduced by half.

2 Whisk stock and flour together in a small jug; stir into beef mixture. Reduce heat to medium; cook, stirring occasionally, for 5 minutes or until sauce has thickened. Season to taste. Transfer filling to a tray; refrigerate until cooled.

3 Preheat oven to 200°C/400°F. Grease 2 x 12-hole (⅓-cup/80ml) muffin pans.

4 Roll shortcrust and puff pastry sheets on a lightly floured surface until 3mm (⅛-inch) thick. Using the 9cm round cutter, cut 24 rounds from shortcrust pastry. Using the 6cm round cutter, cut 24 rounds from puff pastry.

5 To assemble, line pan holes with shortcrust rounds; top equally with cooled beef filling. Brush puff pastry edges with beaten egg. Place pastry, egg-side down, over filling; press edges to seal. Using a small knife, make a small cut in the top of each pie; brush with beaten egg and push the rosemary into the cut. Bake 25 minutes or until pastry is golden and filling is hot.

6 Serve pies immediately on a large platter. Serve with tomato sauce (ketchup), if you like.

tip We used a shiraz-style wine in this recipe.
do-ahead Pies can be made a day ahead, store in an airtight container in the fridge. Reheat, loosely covered with foil, in a 180°C/350°F oven for 12 minutes.

smoked ocean trout and pickled fennel buns

PREP + COOK TIME 20 MINUTES (+ REFRIGERATION) **MAKES** 20

20 medium bread rolls (1kg), halved

1 cup (240g) spreadable cream cheese

2 baby cos lettuce (360g), leaves separated

4 small red radishes (140g), sliced thinly

1 small red onion (100g), sliced thinly into rings

480g (15½ ounces) hot-smoked ocean trout or salmon fillets, flaked

PICKLED FENNEL

⅓ cup (80ml) strained lemon juice

2 tablespoons caster (superfine) sugar

2 tablespoons finely chopped fresh dill

1 tablespoon mustard seeds, toasted

1 tablespoon white wine vinegar

2 teaspoons sea salt flakes

4 baby fennel bulbs (520g), trimmed, sliced thinly

¼ cup (60ml) extra virgin olive oil

1 Make pickled fennel.

2 Spread bread roll bases with cream cheese; layer with lettuce, pickled fennel, radish, onion and trout. Top with bread roll lids.

3 Serve buns immediately on a large platter.

PICKLED FENNEL Whisk juice, sugar, dill, seeds, vinegar and salt until sugar dissolves. Add fennel, season to taste; toss to combine. Cover; refrigerate, 30 minutes to allow flavours to develop. Drain and discard pickling liquid, then toss pickled fennel with olive oil.

---

nutritional count per bun
- ▶ 10g total fat
- ▶ 3.6g saturated fat
- ▶ 1080kJ (258 cal)
- ▶ 3.6g carbohydrate
- ▶ 14.9g protein
- ▶ 0.8g fibre

test kitchen tips

Use a mandoline or V-slicer,
available from kitchenware
and department stores, to
slice the fennel and radishes.
For decoration and ease of
handling either tie the rolls
with kitchen string or secure
them with toothpicks.

test kitchen tip

The pear in this recipe
acts as a tenderiser, the
longer the calamari
marinates the more
tender it will become.

korean barbecued squid on skewers

PREP + COOK TIME 45 MINUTES (+ REFRIGERATION) **MAKES** 50

You need 50 x 18cm (7¼-inch) bamboo skewers.

1kg (2 pounds) cleaned squid hoods

⅓ cup (75g) caster (superfine) sugar

¼ cup (60ml) sake

2 tablespoons fish sauce

3 cloves garlic, crushed

3cm (1¼-inch) piece fresh ginger (15g), grated finely

2 tablespoons shrimp paste

2 tablespoons soya bean and chilli paste

2 tablespoons sesame oil

1 tablespoon cider vinegar

10cm (4-inch) stalk fresh lemon grass (20g), white part only, chopped finely

1 medium green pear (230g), grated coarsely

4 x 3cm (1½-inch) thin strips orange rind

2 fresh long red chillies, seeded, sliced thinly

2 medium lemons (280g), cut into wedges

1 Halve squid hoods lengthways. Using a sharp knife, score inside in a criss-cross pattern at 5mm (¼-inch) intervals. Cut into 4cm x 8cm (1½-inch x 3½-inch) pieces.

2 Place sugar, sake, sauce, garlic, ginger, both pastes, oil, vinegar, lemon grass, pear and rind in a large bowl; whisk to combine. Add squid, season; toss to coat. Cover; refrigerate for 3 hours or overnight.

3 Preheat a lightly oiled grill pan (or barbecue) on high heat. Drain squid; reserve marinade. Thread squid pieces onto skewers in an 'S'-shape. Cook skewers, in batches, turning occasionally and brushing with reserved marinade, for 5 minutes or until cooked through and charred lightly.

4 Place skewers on a large platter; sprinkle over chilli, accompany with lemon wedges.

tip Soak bamboo skewers for at least 30 minutes before using, to prevent burning when cooking.
do-ahead Squid can be marinated a day ahead; store, covered, in the fridge.

nutritional count per skewer
▶ 0.3g total fat
▶ 0.1g saturated fat
▶ 77kJ (18 cal)
▶ 0.3g carbohydrate
▶ 3.3g protein
▶ 0.1g fibre

mustard dogs in pastry

PREP + COOK TIME 35 MINUTES **MAKES** 12

2 sheets puff pastry

½ cup (140g) wholegrain mustard

1 cup (120g) finely grated cheddar

6 american-style hot dogs (390g), halved crossways

1 egg, beaten lightly

2 tablespoons poppy seeds

1 Preheat oven to 220°C/425°F. Line a large oven tray with baking paper.

2 Cut each pastry sheet into 3 x 8cm (3¼-inch) lengths; halve each length crossways into rectangles.

3 Spread 2 teaspoons mustard over each rectangle, sprinkle with 1 tablespoon cheese; leave a 1cm (½-inch) border down one short side. Place one hot dog half over mustard and cheese; roll up tightly.

4 Place mustard dogs, seam-side down, on oven tray, brush with egg; sprinkle with poppy seeds.

5 Bake 15 minutes or until pastry is puffed and golden. Serve immediately.

tip We used the HANS variety because they didn't split.

do-ahead Mustard dogs can be assembled a day ahead; refrigerate covered. Alternately, freeze and store for up to 2 weeks. If cooking from frozen, bake for 25 minutes.

nutritional count per piece
▶ 17.6g total fat   ▶ 16.1g carbohydrate
▶ 8.9g saturated fat   ▶ 10.1g protein
▶ 1107kJ (264 cal)   ▶ 1.1g fibre

chicken, jalapeño and cheese quesadillas

PREP + COOK TIME 30 MINUTES **MAKES** 20

2 cups (320g) shredded, skinless barbecue chicken

1 cup (120g) finely grated cheddar

1 cup (100g) finely grated mozzarella

¼ cup (50g) drained, finely chopped pickled jalapeño chillies

½ medium red onion (85g), sliced thinly

16 x 15cm (6-inch) mini corn or flour tortillas

¼ cup (60ml) olive oil

¾ cup (90g) finely grated cheddar, extra

2 medium avocados (500g)

2 tablespoons lime juice

⅓ cup loosely packed fresh coriander leaves (cilantro)

1 Preheat oven to 180°C/350°F. Line a large oven tray with baking paper.

2 Combine chicken, cheeses, chilli and onion in a large bowl; season to taste. Fold tortilla into quarters. Holding folded tortilla like a cone; divide filling among tortillas. Place a toothpick into the base of each tortilla to hold it closed, if necessary; place on the oven tray.

3 Brush quesadillas with oil; sprinkle over extra cheese. Bake 12 minutes or until golden and heated through.

4 Meanwhile, combine avocado and lime juice in a bowl; season to taste. Sprinskle with coriander.

5 Serve quesadilla on a platter, topped with a tablespoon of the avocado mixture.

nutritional count per piece
▶ 13.8g total fat
▶ 11.3g carbohydrate
▶ 5.5g saturated fat
▶ 9.9g protein
▶ 878kJ (210 cal)
▶ 0.6g fibre

beef and bacon sliders

PREP + COOK TIME 35 MINUTES (+ COOLING & REFRIGERATION) **MAKES** 12

½ cup (125ml) olive oil

5 rindless short-cut bacon slices (175g), cut into matchsticks

1 small red onion (80g), chopped finely

600g (1 pound) thick beef sausages

2 tablespoons finely chopped fresh flat-leaf parsley

12 medium round dinner rolls (600g), halved

1 cup (100g) grated pizza cheese

GREEN APPLE SLAW

2 large green apples (200g), unpeeled

1 cup (80g) finely shredded green cabbage

¼ cup small fresh mint leaves

1 green onion (scallion), sliced thinly on the diagonal

⅓ cup (80ml) coleslaw dressing

1 Heat 2 tablespoons of the oil in a large frying pan over high heat, add bacon and onion; cook, stirring occasionally, for 6 minutes or until bacon has browned and onion is soft. Drain on paper towel; cool completely.

2 Make green apple slaw.

3 Remove casings from sausages; place filling in a large bowl. Add bacon mixture and parsley; mix to combine. Divide beef mixture into 12 equal portions; shape into 10cm (4½-inch) patties (or slightly larger than the bread rolls). Refrigerate 30 minutes or until firm.

4 Heat 2 tablespoons of the oil in a large frying pan over medium-high heat. Add half the patties; cook 3 minutes each side. Drain on paper towel, repeat with remaining oil and patties.

5 Preheat grill (broiler) to high. Place roll bases, cut-side up, on baking trays; place patties on roll bases, sprinkle with cheese. Grill for 2 minutes or until cheese melts.

6 Top patties with slaw; sandwich with roll tops. Place rolls on a large platter; serve immediately.

GREEN APPLE SLAW Cut apple into matchsticks. Place ingredients in a large bowl, season to taste; toss gently to combine.

tips Use wet hands to prevent beef mixture from sticking to hands when shaping the patties. Use a toothpick to secure sliders for serving.
do-ahead Patties can be made a day ahead.

---

nutritional count per slider
- ▶ 31.3g total fat
- ▶ 10.6g saturated fat
- ▶ 2022kJ (483 cal)
- ▶ 30.1g carbohydrate
- ▶ 18.8g protein
- ▶ 4.4g fibre

croque monsieur baguette

croque monsieur baguette

PREP + COOK TIME 15 MINUTES **MAKES** 12

1 french bread stick (500g)

80g (1½ ounces) softened butter

½ cup (125g) dijon mustard

12 slices pancetta (180g)

150g (5 ounces) thinly sliced gruyère cheese

12 baby cornichons, drained

1 Using a serrated knife, cut the bread crossways into 24 slices.
2 Brush one side of each slice with butter; turn slices buttered-side down. Spread tops of all slices with mustard; sandwich pancetta and cheese between slices, keeping the buttered side on the outside.
3 Preheat a large sandwich press. Toast sandwiches for 5 minutes or until golden and cheese is melted.
4 Top with a cornichon, secure with a toothpick. Place on a platter to serve.

tip Substitute sliced prosciutto or ham for the pancetta, if you prefer.
do-ahead Sandwiches can be made 4 hours ahead: store, covered, in the fridge. Reheat on a baking-paper-lined oven tray in a 180°C/350°F oven for 6 minutes or until heated through.

nutritional count per piece
▶ 9.1g total fat   ▶ 26.7g carbohydrate
▶ 4.6g saturated fat   ▶ 10.4g protein
▶ 981kJ (234 cal)   ▶ 1.8g fibre

chimichurri lamb cutlets

PREP + COOK TIME 25 MINUTES (+ REFRIGERATION)
MAKES 20

4 fresh long red chillies, seeded, chopped finely

3 cloves garlic, crushed

2 tablespoons red wine vinegar

2 teaspoons dried oregano

2 teaspoons ground cumin

2 teaspoons sweet paprika

1 large tomato (220g), chopped finely

1 large red onion (200g), chopped finely

½ cup firmly packed fresh flat-leaf parsley leaves, shredded finely

1 cup (250ml) extra virgin olive oil

20 frenched lamb cutlets (1kg)

1 To make chimichurri, place all ingredients except lamb in a large bowl, season; stir to combine.
2 Place half the chimichurri in a large bowl with lamb; toss to coat in marinade. Cover; refrigerate 3 hours or overnight. Cover remaining chimichurri; refrigerate until required.
3 Preheat a grill pan (or barbecue) over high heat. Cook lamb, turning occasionally, for 4 minutes (for medium) or until cooked to your liking. Cover lamb; rest for 5 minutes.
4 Place lamb cutlets on a large platter; serve with reserved chimichurri. Sprinkle over extra fresh parsley sprigs to serve, if you like.

(photograph page 74)

nutritional count per cutlet
▶ 17g total fat   ▶ 1g carbohydrate
▶ 4.3g saturated fat   ▶ 5.5g protein
▶ 747kJ (179 cal)   ▶ 0.7g fibre

test kitchen tips

If you are pressed for time, process all the chimichurri ingredients in a food processor until coarsely chopped. You can substitute chicken wings or drumsticks for the lamb cutlets, if you prefer.

chimichurri lamb cutlets (recipe page 73)

tomato, pancetta and buffalo mozzarella pizza

PREP + COOK TIME 45 MINUTES (+ STANDING) **MAKES** 40

1 cup (250ml) barbecue sauce

250g (8 ounces) mixed baby heirloom tomatoes, halved

10 slices pancetta (150g), torn roughly

3 balls buffalo mozzarella (420g), drained, torn

1 cup loosely packed small fresh basil leaves

PIZZA DOUGH

1½ cups (375ml) warm milk

2 teaspoons (7g) dried yeast

1 tablespoon honey

4 cups (600g) plain (all-purpose) flour

1 teaspoon salt

¼ cup (60ml) extra virgin olive oil

1 Make pizza dough.
2 Preheat oven to 220°C/425°F. Line oven trays with baking paper.
3 Divide pizza dough into 40 balls. Roll each ball on a lightly floured surface into 6cm (2½-inch) rounds. Place pizza bases on oven trays (see tip).
4 Spread 1 teaspoon sauce over each pizza base. Divide tomatoes, pancetta and mozzarella between bases. Bake pizzas, in batches, for 15 minutes or until bases are crisp and mozzarella melted.
5 Sprinkle pizzas with basil. Serve immediately.

PIZZA DOUGH Combine milk, yeast and honey in a small bowl. Stand for 5 minutes or until foamy. Combine flour and salt in a large bowl; make a well in the centre, add yeast mixture and oil. Using your hands, mix until combined. Turn dough onto a lightly floured surface; knead for 10 minutes or until dough is smooth and elastic. Place in an oiled bowl, turn to coat in oil. Cover with plastic wrap; stand in a warm, draught-free place for 1 hour or until dough is doubled in size.

nutritional count per pizza
▶ 4.8g total fat
▶ 2.2g saturated fat
▶ 548kJ (130 cal)
▶ 15.6g carbohydrate
▶ 5.9g protein
▶ 0.7g fibre

test kitchen tip

If you don't have enough oven trays to bake the pizzas, roll out the dough on sheets of baking paper and carefully transfer the paper with the pizzas to hot trays (from the previous batch). You may need to reduce the cooking time by a few minutes.

sesame-crusted chicken goujons

PREP + COOK TIME 35 MINUTES **MAKES** 32

Goujons are small strips of fish or chicken (as we use here), coated in breadcrumbs and deep-fried.

1 cup (150g) plain (all-purpose) flour

3 eggs

1 tablespoon water

2 cups (150g) japanese breadcrumbs (panko)

½ cup (50g) white sesame seeds

½ cup (50g) black sesame seeds

1kg (2 pounds) chicken breast fillets, sliced thickly on the diagonal

vegetable oil, for shallow-frying

2 limes, halved and cut into thin wedges, to serve

WASABI MAYONNAISE

1 cup (300g) whole-egg mayonnaise

1½ tablespoons wasabi paste

1 tablespoon finely chopped coriander (cilantro)

1 teaspoon mirin

1 Make wasabi mayonnaise.
2 Place flour in a shallow bowl; season. In another shallow bowl, lightly beat eggs with the water. Place breadcrumbs and sesame seeds in a third shallow bowl; toss to combine. Coat chicken strips in flour, dip in egg, allow excess to drip off, then coat in breadcrumb mixture.
3 Heat 1cm (½-inch) oil in a large frying pan over medium heat. Cook chicken, in batches, turning frequently, for 3½ minutes or until golden and cooked through. Remove with a slotted spoon; drain on paper towel.
4 Serve chicken with mayonnaise and lime wedges.

WASABI MAYONNAISE Place ingredients in a small bowl; stir to combine. Season to taste.

nutritional count per piece

▶ 13.8g total fat
▶ 2.2g saturated fat
▶ 808kJ (193 cal)
▶ 7.6g carbohydrate
▶ 9.6g protein
▶ 0.5g fibre

tempura prawns with lime and chilli sauce

PREP + COOK TIME 35 MINUTES (+ REFRIGERATION) **MAKES** 30

1 cup (220g) caster (superfine) sugar

¼ cup (60ml) chinese cooking wine

1 lebanese cucumber (130g), seeded, chopped finely

2 fresh long red chillies, seeded, sliced thinly

2 tablespoons rice wine vinegar

1 tablespoon sesame oil

2 tablespoons lime juice

1 teaspoon finely grated lime rind

250g (8 ounces) tempura batter mix

1¾ cups (330ml) chilled sparkling water

30 medium green king prawns (1.5kg), cleaned, tails intact

vegetable oil, for deep-frying

1 To make lime and chilli sauce: place sugar and wine in a small saucepan over medium heat. Bring to a simmer; cook, stirring, for 5 minutes or until sugar dissolves. Remove from heat; cool slightly. Stir in cucumber and chillies; refrigerate until cooled completely. Stir in vinegar, oil, juice and rind.

2 Meanwhile place tempura mix in a large bowl, season; gradually whisk in sparkling water.

3 Fill a deep-fryer or large saucepan one-third full with vegetable oil; heat over medium heat to 180°C/350°F (or until a cube of bread turns golden in 10 seconds). Dip prawns, in batches, into batter, drain away excess. Deep-fry prawns, turning halfway through cooking time, for 5 minutes or until golden. Remove with a slotted spoon; drain on paper towel.

4 Serve prawns on a large platter; accompany with lime and chilli sauce.

tip Tempura batter mix is available from larger supermarkets in the spice and sauce aisle.

nutritional count per prawn
- ▶ 1.8g total fat
- ▶ 0.3g saturated fat
- ▶ 397kJ (95 cal)
- ▶ 14.2g carbohydrate
- ▶ 5.7g protein
- ▶ 0.1g fibre

79

LITTLE BOXES

smoky barbecued pork ribs

PREP + COOK TIME 1½ HOURS (+ REFRIGERATION) SERVES 10

¾ cup (270g) honey

1½ tablespoons smoked paprika

1½ tablespoons wholegrain mustard

1½ cups (420g) HP sauce

¼ cup (55g) brown sugar

2 cloves garlic, crushed

3kg (6½ pounds) american-style pork ribs, cut into racks of 5

1 Place honey, paprika, mustard, sauce, sugar and garlic in a large bowl; stir to combine. Add ribs to marinade; rub marinade all over ribs to coat. Cover; refrigerate 2 hours to allow flavours to penetrate.
2 Preheat oven to 180°C/350°F. Line a large roasting pan with baking paper (you may need to use two, depending on the size).
3 Place ribs and marinade in baking pan; cover with foil. Bake 1 hour.
4 Remove ribs from oven; brush ribs with marinade from base of pan. Increase oven temperature to 220°C/425°F. Roast ribs, uncovered, for a further 2 minutes, basting occasionally, or until dark and sticky.
5 To serve, cut into individual ribs; place 5 ribs into each container or box.

do-ahead Ribs can be prepared up to the end of step 3; store, covered, in the fridge.

test kitchen tip

Ask the butcher to cut the ribs into lots of 5 when you buy them, or you can do it yourself using poultry shears; cut between each bone to separate into smaller racks.

nutritional count per serving

▶ 11.9g total fat
▶ 4.5g saturated fat
▶ 1573kJ (376 cal)
▶ 38.9g carbohydrate
▶ 28.7g protein
▶ 0.6g fibre

prawn pad thai

PREP + COOK TIME 1 HOUR (+ STANDING) SERVES 12

2 tablespoons small dried shrimps

400g (12½ ounces) dried rice noodles

⅓ cup (80ml) peanut or vegetable oil

¼ cup (60ml) boiling water

½ cup (135g) grated palm sugar

1 tablespoon tamarind puree (concentrate)

¼ cup (60ml) lime juice

⅓ cup (80ml) fish sauce

2 tablespoons soy sauce

800g (1½ pounds) uncooked medium
king prawns (shrimp)

⅔ cup (100g) roasted unsalted peanuts

3 cloves garlic, crushed

1 fresh long red chilli, chopped finely

3 eggs, beaten lightly

6 green onions, sliced thinly diagonally

½ cup (40g) fried asian shallots

150g (4½ ounces) bean sprouts

1 cup firmly packed coriander leaves (cilantro)

2 limes, each cut into 6 wedges

1 Place shrimp in a small heatproof bowl, cover with boiling water; stand 30 minutes until softened. Drain; chop finely. Place noodles in a large heatproof bowl; cover with boiling water. Stand 15 minutes or until just tender. Drain noodles, toss with 2 teaspoons of the oil; cover with plastic wrap to prevent drying out.
2 Stir the boiling water, sugar, tamarind, juice and sauces in a small jug or bowl until sugar dissolves.
3 Peel and devein prawns, leaving tails intact. Chop half the nuts coarsely; chop remaining nuts finely.
4 Heat a wok over high heat; add 1 tablespoon of the oil. Add prawns; stir-fry for 2 minutes or until just beginning to change colour; remove from wok.
5 Add remaining oil, shrimp, garlic and chilli to wok; stir-fry 1 minute or until garlic is fragrant. Add egg; stir-fry 1 minute or until just set. Add noodles, prawns, three-quarters of the green onion and sauce mixture; stir-fry until noodles are heated through.

6 Remove from heat; sprinkle over finely chopped peanuts and half the shallots; toss to combine.
7 Divide pad thai between 12 x 1-cup containers or boxes. Combine coarsely chopped peanuts, bean sprouts, remaining green onion and shallot, and coriander in a medium bowl; sprinkle over pad thai; serve with wedges.

do-ahead Recipe can be prepared 4 hours ahead up to the end of step 4.

nutritional count per 1-cup serving
▶ 12.6g total fat
▶ 2.4g saturated fat
▶ 1213kJ (290 cal)
▶ 29.2g carbohydrate
▶ 14g protein
▶ 0.7g fibre

nutritional count per 1-cup serving
▶ 9.6g total fat
▶ 1.9g saturated fat
▶ 737kJ (176 cal)
▶ 16.3g carbohydrate
▶ 5g protein
▶ 2.3g fibre

chicken and watercress pasta salad

PREP + COOK TIME 30 MINUTES **SERVES** 24

500g (1 pound) small pasta shells

¾ cup (60g) flaked natural almonds

180g (5½ ounces) green beans, trimmed, sliced diagonally

2 cups (240g) frozen peas

3 cups (480g) shredded barbecue chicken

4 cups (200g) firmly packed watercress sprigs

120g (4 ounces) fresh goat's cheese, crumbled

LEMON AND WATERCRESS DRESSING

⅔ cup (160ml) extra virgin olive oil

2 tablespoons white wine vinegar

1 tablespoon lemon juice

1 cup loosely packed fresh flat-leaf parsley leaves

100g (2 cups) watercress sprigs

2 tablespoons finely grated lemon rind

1 Cook pasta in a large saucepan of boiling water for 1 minute less than packet instructions state, or until pasta is slightly firmer than al dente. Drain; rinse under cold running water, drain.

2 Meanwhile, make lemon and watercress dressing.

3 Place almonds, in a single layer, in a dry frying pan; cook over a medium-low heat, stirring constantly, until fragrant and just changed in colour. Remove from pan immediately to stop nuts over-browning or burning.

4 Meanwhile, boil, steam or microwave beans and peas, separately, until vegetables are just tender. Drain; refresh in a bowl of iced water; drain and transfer to a large bowl.

5 Add chicken, pasta and watercress to bowl with vegetables; drizzle over the dressing, toss well to combine. Divide salad among 24 x 1-cup containers sprinkle each with goat's cheese to serve.

LEMON AND WATERCRESS DRESSING Blend or process ingredients until smooth; season to taste.

tips You could substitute spiralli or fusilli for the pasta shells. You will need 2 bunches of watercress. For a cleaner look, arrange ingredients separately in containers, then drizzle with dressing.
do-ahead Recipe can be prepared 8 hours ahead up to the end of step 4.

potato and pork sausage salad

PREP + COOK TIME 45 MINUTES **SERVES** 12

1 bulb garlic

2 tablespoons olive oil

1kg (2 pounds) mixed baby red and yellow potatoes, skin on, sliced thinly

2 tablespoons white wine vinegar

500g (1 pound) pork and fennel sausages

1 cup (300g) whole-egg mayonnaise

2 tablespoons lemon juice

½ cup (50g) rinsed, drained baby capers

100g (3 ounces) cornichons, chopped finely

4 shallots (100g), sliced thinly

1 cup loosely packed fresh flat-leaf parsley, coarsely chopped

⅓ cup coarsely chopped fresh dill

1 Preheat oven to 200°C/400°F.
2 Place garlic in a small shallow baking dish; drizzle with half the oil. Roast garlic for 20 minutes.
3 Meanwhile, boil, steam or microwave potato until just tender. Drain, transfer to a large heatproof bowl; sprinkle with vinegar. Cover to keep warm.
4 Heat remaining oil in a large frying pan on stove top; cook sausages, for 2 minutes or until browned lightly. Transfer to a baking dish with garlic; roast, in oven, a further 10 minutes or until sausages are cooked through and garlic is soft. Cool sausages 10 minutes; slice thinly diagonally.
5 Cut garlic in half horizontally, squeeze flesh into a small bowl; add mayonnaise and juice, mash with a fork. Combine sausages and remaining ingredients with potato; toss well, season to taste. Divide potato salad among 12 x 1-cup boxes or containers; top with garlic mayonnaise.

do-ahead Potato salad can be made 8 hours ahead, minus the sausages; store, covered, in the fridge.

---

nutritional count per 1-cup serving
▶ 33.4g total fat
▶ 15.5g carbohydrate
▶ 8.5g saturated fat
▶ 9.9g protein
▶ 1707kJ (408 cal)
▶ 3.7g fibre

heirloom tomato and mozzarella salad

PREP + COOK TIME 25 MINUTES **SERVES** 12

2 x 125g (4 ounces) long sourdough bread rolls

1 clove garlic, halved

¼ cup (60ml) olive oil

850g (1¾ pounds) small heirloom tomatoes

220g (7 ounces) mozzarella

BASIL AND LEMON OIL DRESSING

1 clove garlic, crushed

1 cup firmly packed fresh basil leaves

1 teaspoon white (granulated) sugar

¼ cup (60ml) white balsamic vinegar

½ cup (125ml) lemon-infused extra virgin olive oil

1 Make basil and lemon oil dressing.

2 Cut bread into 5mm (¼-inch) thick slices; rub both sides with cut side of garlic; brush with olive oil. Cook on a hot grill pan (or toast under grill/broiler) until browned lightly.

3 Cut tomatoes into halves and quarters. Tear cheese into small pieces (or slice thinly).

4 Just before serving, combine tomato, cheese, toast, any remaining olive oil and dressing in a large bowl; toss to combine. Divide salad among 12 x 1-cup containers or boxes; sprinkle over extra fresh small basil leaves to serve, if you like.

BASIL AND LEMON OIL DRESSING Blend or process ingredients until smooth; season to taste.

tip Lemon-infused extra-virgin olive oil is available from major supermarkets. Substitute regular extra-virgin olive oil and ½ teaspoon finely grated lemon rind, if you prefer.
do-ahead Dressing can be prepared 8 hours ahead; store, covered, in the fridge.

nutritional count per 1-cup serving

▶ 19.8g total fat   ▶ 12.4g carbohydrate
▶ 5.1g saturated fat   ▶ 7.4g protein
▶ 1092kJ (260 cal)   ▶ 1g fibre

little green thai chicken curries

PREP + COOK TIME 50 MINUTES **SERVES** 12

1½ cups (300g) jasmine rice

3 cups (750ml) water

¾ cup (30g) flaked coconut

2 tablespoons peanut or vegetable oil

800g (1½ pounds) chicken thigh fillets, trimmed

100g (3 ounces) green curry paste

1 clove garlic, crushed

4cm (1½-inch) piece fresh ginger (20g), finely grated

225g (7 ounces) canned bamboo shoots, rinsed, drained

400g (12½ ounces) canned coconut cream

200g (6½ ounces) snow peas, trimmed, sliced thinly diagonally

1 tablespoon lime juice

1 cup coriander leaves (cilantro)

2 small red thai (serrano) chillies, halved, sliced thinly

1 Place rice in a sieve; rinse under running water until water runs clear. Place rice and the water in a medium saucepan; bring to the boil over medium heat. Reduce heat to low, cover with lid; cook for 12 minutes or until most of the water is absorbed. Stand, covered, for 10 minutes.

2 Meanwhile, place coconut in a medium frying pan; cook, stirring over high heat, for 4 minutes or until golden. Transfer to a medium bowl; cool.

3 Heat half the oil in a large wok over high heat. Add half the chicken; stir-fry for 4 minutes or until browned and just cooked. Remove from wok. Repeat with remaining oil and chicken. Slice thinly; cover to keep warm.

4 Add curry paste, garlic and ginger to wok; stir-fry for 2 minutes or until heated through. Add bamboo shoots and coconut cream; bring to the boil. Reduce heat; simmer 3 minutes or until sauce thickens. Return chicken to wok. Stir in snow peas and lime juice; stir-fry for a further 2 minutes.

5 Divide rice and curry between small boxes or containers, allowing ⅓ cup for each. Combine coriander, chilli and coconut in a small bowl; sprinkle over curry to serve.

tip To make the curry go further, add an extra 200g each of trimmed green beans and fresh baby corn.

do-ahead All curry ingredients can be weighed and prepared up to 8 hours ahead; store, covered, in the fridge. Rice can be cooked 8 hours ahead; however, care must be taken to refrigerate it immediately after cooking and to reheat it thoroughly, since rice can harbour dangerous bacteria if not handled correctly.

nutritional count per 1-cup serving
▶ 23.4g total fat
▶ 11.2g saturated fat
▶ 1512kJ (361 cal)
▶ 23.6g carbohydrate
▶ 13.5g protein
▶ 1.2g fibre

poached ocean trout salad with japanese dressing

PREP + COOK TIME 35 MINUTES **SERVES** 20

1½ cups (375ml) fish stock

2 cups (500ml) water

4 x 200g (6½ ounces) skinless ocean trout fillets

340g (11 ounces) asparagus, trimmed, sliced thickly diagonally

160g (5 ounces) green beans, trimmed, cut into 2cm (¾-inch) lengths

2 tablespoons sesame seeds

500g (1 pound) small red radishes, trimmed

1 medium telegraph (hothouse) cucumber (400g)

200g (6½ ounces) baby spinach leaves

200g (6½ ounces) mizuna leaves

JAPANESE DRESSING

6cm (2½-inch) piece fresh ginger (30g), finely grated

¼ cup (60ml) olive oil

2 tablespoons lime juice

¼ cup (60ml) mirin

¼ cup (60ml) soy sauce

1 tablespoon finely grated palm sugar

1 small red thai (serrano) chilli, chopped finely

1 Place stock and the water in a medium saucepan; bring to the boil over medium heat. Reduce heat to a simmer; add fish fillets, cook for 8 minutes or until almost cooked through. Using a slotted spoon, transfer fish to plate; cool 5 minutes.

2 Meanwhile, return poaching liquid to the boil, add asparagus and beans; cook for 30 seconds or until asparagus is just tender. Drain; refresh in iced water, then drain again.

3 Make japanese dressing.

4 Place sesame seeds in a small frying pan over medium heat; stir continuously for 2 minutes or until golden. Remove from heat immediately.

5 Thinly slice radishes. Halve, seed and thinly slice cucumber diagonally. Place cucumber and radish in a large bowl; add spinach, mizuna and vegetables. Flake fish, add to salad; drizzle with the dressing. Divide salad among 20 x 1-cup boxes or containers. Sprinkle with sesame seeds to serve.

JAPANESE DRESSING Combine ingredients in a small screw-top jar; shake well.

tip Substitute watercress and tatsoi leaves for baby spinach and mizuna, if preferred.

do-ahead Recipe can be prepared 8 hours ahead to the end of step 4; store, covered, in the fridge.

nutritional count per 1-cup serving
▶ 7.9g total fat
▶ 1.8g saturated fat
▶ 560kJ (134 cal)
▶ 3.7g carbohydrate
▶ 10.8g protein
▶ 1.4g fibre

five-spice squid with lime mayonnaise

PREP + COOK TIME 40 MINUTES SERVES 24

2 tablespoons chinese five spice

1 tablespoon ground ginger

1 teaspoon sea salt flakes, crushed

3 teaspoons onion powder

2 tablespoons self-raising flour

½ cup (75g) cornflour (cornstarch)

600g (1¼ pounds) cleaned small squid (hoods and tentacles)

vegetable oil, for deep-frying

4 green onions (scallions), sliced thinly diagonally

2 fresh long red chillies, sliced thinly diagonally

4 limes, each cut into 6 wedges

LIME MAYONNAISE

2 teaspoons finely grated lime rind

2 teaspoons lime juice

2 cups (600g) japanese mayonnaise

1 Make lime mayonnaise.

2 Combine spices, salt and onion powder in a large bowl; reserve one-third of spice mixture. Add flours to remaining mixture; stir to combine.

3 Cut each squid hood in half lengthways. Score inside in a criss-cross pattern with a sharp knife, then cut into 1.5cm (½-inch) wide strips.

4 Fill a large wok one-third full with oil; heat to 180°C/350°F (or until a cube of bread turns golden in 10 seconds). Working in batches, toss squid and tentacles in flour spice mix; shake away excess. Fry squid for 2 minutes or until golden and just tender; drain on paper towel. Transfer to a large bowl.

5 Fry onion and chilli for 2 minutes or until golden. Using a slotted spoon, remove from oil, add to bowl with squid; toss well to combine.

6 Divide squid into ¼-cup serving cones. Sprinkle with reserved spice mix to serve; accompany with lime mayonnaise and lime wedges.

LIME MAYONNAISE Combine ingredients in a small bowl. Cover, refrigerate until ready to serve.

do-ahead Recipe can be prepared a day ahead up to the end of step 3; store, covered, in the fridge.

nutritional count per ¼-cup serving
▶ 22g total fat
▶ 3.9g saturated fat
▶ 987kJ (236 cal)
▶ 4.3g carbohydrate
▶ 4.6g protein
▶ 0.2g fibre

test kitchen tips

Japanese mayonnaise, from Asian grocers and selected supermarkets, is made with rice vinegar and has a slightly different taste from regular mayonnaise, which may be substituted. To clean squid, gently pull head and tentacles with internal sac away from body. Remove clear cartilage (quill) from inside body. Cut tentacles from head just below the eyes; discard head. Remove and discard side fins and skin from body with salted fingers. Wash the body and tentacles thoroughly; pat dry.

nutritional count per serving
▶ 28.4g total fat
▶ 6.3g saturated fat
▶ 2109kJ (504 cal)
▶ 32.8g carbohydrate
▶ 24.4g protein
▶ 2.3g fibre

test kitchen tip

If you can find it, use a short-grain Spanish-style rice such as calasparra or bomba, in place of the arborio for an authentic taste and texture.

paella with garlic aïoli

PREP + COOK TIME 50 MINUTES **SERVES** 12

1 litre (4 cups) chicken stock

12 saffron threads

¼ cup (60ml) olive oil

3 chicken thigh fillets (600g), trimmed, cut into 2cm (¾-inch) pieces

2 cured chorizo sausages (340g), sliced thinly diagonally

1 large brown onion (200g), chopped finely

1 large red capsicum (bell pepper) (350g), chopped finely

2 teaspoons smoked paprika

2 cloves garlic, crushed

2 large tomatoes (440g), seeded, chopped finely

2 cups (400g) arborio rice

12 small black mussels (300g), scrubbed, bearded

12 large uncooked king prawns (840g), shelled, deveined, with tails intact

½ cup (60g) frozen peas

½ cup coarsely chopped fresh flat-leaf parsley

¾ cup (225g) garlic aïoli

2 medium lemons (280g), cut into 12 wedges

1 Place stock in a small saucepan; bring to the boil over medium heat. Add saffron, cover to keep warm.
2 Heat 2 tablespoons of the oil in a 38cm (15¼-inch) paella or two 20cm (8-inch) frying pans over medium heat. Add chicken and chorizo; cook for 2 minutes each side or until browned. Remove from pan.
3 Add remaining oil to pan, add onion, capsicum and paprika; cook, stirring, for 5 minutes or until softened. Add garlic; stir for 1 minute. Add tomato and rice, stir for 1 minute or until grains are well coated in mixture. Return chicken and chorizo to pan. Pour stock and saffron mixture into pan; bring to the boil. Reduce heat to medium-low, cook 10 minutes or until rice has absorbed most of the liquid.
4 Push mussels into hot rice mixture. Scatter over prawns, cover loosely with foil; cook for a further 5 minutes or until mussels open and rice is tender.
5 Sprinkle over peas, cover with foil; stand paella for 5 minutes (the residual heat will finish cooking the paella and peas).
6 To serve, divide paella between 12 x 14cm (5½-inch) mini round pans (2cm/¾-inch deep). Sprinkle with parsley; top each with 2 teaspoons garlic aïoli and a lemon wedge.

tip Some mussels might not open after cooking. These might need to be opened with a knife or might not have cooked as quickly as the others – some will not open after excessive cooking – you do not have to discard these, just open with a knife and cook a little more if you wish.

do-ahead All ingredients can be prepared 8 hours ahead; store, covered, in the fridge. Cooking is best done just before serving.

SWEET THINGS

black forest brownies with cherry chocolate ganache

PREP + COOK TIME 1 HOUR (+ STANDING & REFRIGERATION) MAKES 24

½ cup (100g) bottled amarena cherries in syrup

125g (4 ounces) butter, chopped

185g (6 ounces) dark (semi-sweet) chocolate, chopped coarsely

1 cup (220g) caster (superfine) sugar

¼ cup (60ml) water

2 eggs, beaten lightly

1 cup (150g) plain (all-purpose) flour

24 fresh cherries (175g)

CHERRY CHOCOLATE GANACHE

½ cup (125m) pouring cream

⅓ cup (80ml) amarena cherry syrup (from the cherries in syrup in the brownie)

220g (7 ounces) dark chocolate (70% cocoa), chopped coarsely

1 Preheat oven to 180°C/350°F. Grease 20cm x 30cm (8-inch x 12-inch) slice pan; line base with paper, extending paper 5cm (2-inches) above long sides.
2 Drain cherries, reserving syrup for the cherry chocolate ganache. Chop cherries coarsely.
3 Place butter and chocolate in a small saucepan; stir over low heat until melted. Transfer to a large bowl. Stir in sugar and the water, then eggs, sifted flour and amarena cherries. Pour mixture into pan.
4 Bake 30 minutes or until set; cool brownie in pan.
5 Meanwhile, make cherry chocolate ganache.
6 Turn brownie, top-side up, into serving plate. Spread ganache over brownie; cut into 24 pieces. Top each piece with a fresh cherry to serve.

CHERRY CHOCOLATE GANACHE Heat cream and syrup in a small saucepan until almost boiling, add chocolate; whisk until smooth. Refrigerate for 1 hour or until ganache is a spreadable consistency.

do-ahead Brownie can be made a day ahead up to the end of step 4; store, covered, in the fridge.

test kitchen tips

You need 2 x 240g (7½-ounce) bottles of amarena cherries. Unlike maraschino and glacé cherries, which are bleached and dyed red, Italian amarena cherries are a small sour cherry preserved in sugar syrup to retain their natural garnet colour and cherry taste. They are available from speciality delis and good greengrocers.

nutritional count per piece

▶ 11.4g total fat
▶ 7g saturated fat
▶ 885kJ (211 cal)
▶ 25.8g carbohydrate
▶ 2.3g protein
▶ 0.6g fibre

little portuguese tarts

PREP + COOK TIME 45 MINUTES (+ STANDING) **MAKES** 36

You need 3 x 12-hole (2 tablespoons/40ml) deep flat-based patty pans. If you only have one pan, wash it in cold water to cool it between baking the tart cases (dry pan before re-using).

1½ tablespoons ground cinnamon

1 cup (220g) caster (superfine) sugar

3 sheets butter puff pastry

4 egg yolks

2 tablespoons cornflour (cornstarch)

2 tablespoons custard powder

2¼ cups (560ml) milk

½ teaspoon vanilla extract

½ cup (80g) icing (confectioners') sugar

1 Preheat oven to 200°C/400°F. Grease 3 x 12-hole (2 tablespoons/40ml) deep flat-based patty pans.

2 Combine cinnamon and ¼ cup of the sugar in a small bowl. Sprinkle each pastry sheet well with cinnamon sugar. Roll each sheet up tightly; cut into 12 equal-sized rounds. Place rounds cut-side down. Roll each round into a circle with a diameter of 9cm (3¾-inch); using your fingers, press rounds into pan holes ensuring pastry is pressed firmly into the base of the pan. Freeze for 5 minutes.

3 Whisk remaining sugar, egg yolks, cornflour and custard powder in a medium bowl until light and fluffy. Combine milk and vanilla in a medium saucepan; bring mixture almost to the boil. Whisking continuously, gradually pour milk mixture into egg mixture; return custard mixture to same saucepan.

Cook custard over low heat, stirring continuously, until mixture boils and thickens; remove from heat. Transfer mixture to a large jug.

4 Pour custard mixture equally between cases (about 1 tablespoon each); bake 15 minutes or until pastry is golden and custard just set; cool.

5 Just before serving, dust cooled tarts with sifted icing sugar. Using a kitchen blowtorch, caramelise the tops of the tarts.

tip If you don't have a kitchen blowtorch, sprinkle the sifted icing sugar over the top of the tarts before baking, then bake as per step 4.

nutritional count per tart
- ▶ 4.6g total fat
- ▶ 2.6g saturated fat
- ▶ 468kJ (112 cal)
- ▶ 16.1g carbohydrate
- ▶ 1.7g protein
- ▶ 0.2g fibre

test kitchen tip

Gently swirl the gold leaf
into the jelly to distribute
it throughout before
placing it into the fridge.

prosecco and raspberry jellies

prosecco and raspberry jellies

PREP + COOK TIME 35 MINUTES (+ REFRIGERATION)
MAKES 12

4 teaspoons powdered gelatine

½ cup (125ml) water

½ cup (125ml) blood orange juice

⅔ cup (110g) caster (superfine) sugar

750ml (25 fluid-ounce) bottle prosecco (Italian sparkling wine), chilled

12 raspberries (50g)

1 sheet edible gold leaf

1 Sprinkle gelatine over the water in a small heatproof jug; stand jug in a small saucepan of simmering water. Stir until gelatine dissolves; cool 5 minutes.
2 Heat juice and sugar in a small saucepan, stirring until sugar dissolves. Bring to the boil; remove from heat. Stir in gelatine mixture and prosecco. Strain jelly mixture through a fine sieve into a large jug.
3 Place 16 x ¼-cup (60ml) glasses on a tray. Divide jelly mixture between glasses; add 1 raspberry to each jelly.
4 Using a skewer, to prevent gold leaf from sticking to your hands, carefully tear off pieces of gold leaf; gently stir pieces through jelly. Refrigerate for 6 hours or overnight until set.

tip Edible gold leaf is available from cake decorating supply shops. Alternatively, top the jellies with tiny scoops of ice-cream.
do-ahead Jellies can be made a day ahead; store, covered, in the fridge.

nutritional count per jelly
▶ 0g total fat   ▶ 11.9g carbohydrate
▶ 0g saturated fat   ▶ 1.1g protein
▶ 360kJ (86 cal)   ▶ 0.3g fibre

elderflower and cranberry ice-pops

PREP + COOK TIME 25 MINUTES (+ FREEZING)
MAKES 24

Ice-pops are best prepared 1 day ahead. You need 24 x ¼-cup (60ml) ice-pop moulds and 24 ice-block sticks (see tips, below).

⅓ cup (80ml) vodka

½ cup (125ml) elderflower cordial

2 tablespoons (40ml) strained lime juice

1 cup (250ml) sparking mineral water

2 tablespoons fresh mint leaves, thinly sliced

3 cups (750ml) cranberry juice

1 Combine vodka, cordial, lime juice and mineral water in a medium jug. Divide mixture between the moulds; sprinkle equally with mint. Wrap the mould completely in plastic wrap; insert the ice-block sticks into holes, piercing the plastic. (The plastic wrap will help keep the sticks upright.) Freeze for 6 hours or until mixture is frozen.
2 Pour cranberry juice over the vodka mint layer. Freeze for 2 hours or until juice is frozen.
3 Just before serving, rub the outside of the moulds with a hot kitchen cloth; gently remove ice-pops.

tips The ice-pops can be make several days ahead. Instead of ice-block moulds, we used ¼-cup shot glasses and lollypop sticks.

(photograph page 102)

nutritional count per ice-pop
▶ 0g total fat   ▶ 7.8g carbohydrate
▶ 0g saturated fat   ▶ 0.1g protein
▶ 161kJ (39 cal)   ▶ 0g fibre

elderflower and cranberry ice-pops (recipe page 101)

strawberry toffee pops

PREP + COOK TIME 55 MINUTES (+ STANDING) **MAKES** 16

You need 16 x 15cm (6-inch) lollipop sticks or bamboo skewers.

16 large strawberries (480g)
1 cup (80g) flaked almonds, toasted
2 cups (440g) white (granulated) sugar
1 cup (250ml) water
180g (5½ ounces) dark chocolate Melts

1 Push lollipop sticks or skewers, through the green top, three-quarters of the way into the top of each strawberry.

2 Finely chop nuts; place in a small bowl. Line a work surface with a long sheet of baking paper.

3 Combine sugar and the water in a small saucepan, stir over low heat until sugar dissolves. Bring to a boil; boil, without stirring, for 15 minutes or until golden caramel in colour. Remove from heat; allow bubbles to subside.

4 Working quickly, dip strawberries, one at a time, into caramel mixture, allowing excess to drip off, then place on baking paper; stand until set.

5 Meanwhile, melt chocolate in a small heatproof bowl over a small saucepan of simmering water (don't let the water touch base of bowl). Dip the caramel-coated strawberries into melted chocolate; allow excess chocolate to drip away, then sprinkle with nuts. Place on baking paper; stand until set.

tip Strawberries are at their best served just after being dipped. They are not suitable to refrigerate as the caramel will liquefy.

nutritional count per pop
▸ 6g total fat
▸ 35.6g carbohydrate
▸ 2g saturated fat
▸ 2.1g protein
▸ 838kJ (200 cal)
▸ 0.6g fibre

sumac strawberry meringue nests

PREP + COOK TIME 1¼ HOURS (+ COOLING & REFRIGERATION) MAKES 20

4 egg whites, at room temperature

1 cup (220g) caster (superfine) sugar

1 tablespoon cornflour (cornstarch)

2 teaspoons white vinegar

250g (8 ounces) strawberries, thinly sliced into rounds (see tip)

⅓ cup (55g) icing (confectioners') sugar

1½ tablespoons sumac

300ml thickened (heavy) cream

1 teaspoon vanilla extract

1 Preheat oven to 120°C/250°F. Grease 3 oven trays; line with baking paper.

2 Whisk egg whites in a small bowl with an electric mixer until soft peaks form; gradually add caster sugar, 1 tablespoon at a time, beating until sugar dissolves between additions. Gently fold in sifted cornflour and vinegar. Using 2 spoons; spoon 2 tablespoonfuls of meringue in mounds onto trays. Using the back of a spoon, create an indent in the centre of each mound for the filling.

3 Bake meringues for 40 minutes or until firm to the touch. Cool in oven with door ajar.

4 Meanwhile, combine strawberries, sifted icing sugar and 1 tablespoon of the sumac in a small bowl; cover, refrigerate for 3 hours.

5 Just before serving, whisk cream and vanilla in a small bowl with an electric mixer until firm peaks form. Spoon cream equally among meringues, top with sumac strawberries; sprinkle with remaining sumac to serve.

tip Don't slice the strawberries too thinly or they will fall apart during refrigeration.

nutritional count per nest

▶ 5.6g total fat ▶ 15.2g carbohydrate

▶ 3.6g saturated fat ▶ 1.2g protein

▶ 476kJ (113 cal) ▶ 0.1g fibre

rosewater and pistachio cheesecake cups

PREP + COOK TIME 55 MINUTES (+ COOLING) **SERVES** 16

100g (3 ounces) pistachios

½ cup (110g) caster (superfine) sugar

½ teaspoon ground cinnamon

½ teaspoon ground cardamom

6 sheets fillo pastry, cut in half crossways

50g (1½ ounces) butter, melted

2¼ cups (360g) icing (confectioners') sugar

750g (1½ pounds) cream cheese, softened

2 tablespoons rosewater

¼ cup (60ml) lemon juice

1½ teaspoons lemon rind

¾ cup (180g) pomegranate seeds

100g (3 ounces) rose-flavoured persian fairy floss

1 Preheat oven to 180°C/350°F. Line two oven trays with baking paper.

2 Place nuts on one oven tray; roast for 5 minutes or until browned lightly. Transfer to a food processor; cool. Process cooled nuts until ground finely. Tip into a small bowl, add caster sugar and spices; stir to combine. Wash oven tray to cool; re-line with the baking paper.

3 Place one pastry half on each oven tray; lightly brush with melted butter, sprinkle ¼ cup nut spice mixture between the two pastry halves. Repeat the layering with pastry halves, butter and nut mixture. Top with remaining pastry halves; brush with the remaining butter and sprinkle with remaining nut mixture. Bake 15 minutes or until pastry is golden; cool. Crumble pastry into small pieces; keep in an airtight container until needed.

4 Beat sifted icing sugar, cream cheese, rosewater, juice and rind in a small bowl with electric mixer until soft peaks form.

5 Spoon ¼-cups of cream cheese mixture into ¾-cup (180ml) glasses; sprinkle with the crumbled pastry and pomegranate seeds. Top with fairy floss, just before serving.

tip Persian fairy floss, also known as pashmak, is from delis and specialist cookware shops.
do-ahead Cheesecake cups can be assembled several hours ahead without the fairy floss; store, covered, in the fridge.

nutritional count per ¾-cup serving
▶ 13.6g total fat
▶ 6.7g saturated fat
▶ 1243kJ (297 cal)
▶ 40.9g carbohydrate
▶ 4g protein
▶ 0.5g fibre

test kitchen tip

To remove pomegranate seeds, cut the pomegranate in half, and use your fingers (or gloves, as the juice will stain your hands) to scrape the seeds from the flesh whilst holding the pomegranate upside down in a bowl of cold water; the seeds will sink and the white pith will float to the surface. Discard the pith, and drain the seeds before using.

drunken mocha mousse tartlets

PREP + COOK TIME 55 MINUTES (+ COOLING & REFRIGERATION) **MAKES** 24

You need a 9cm (3¾-inch) round cutter and
24 x 4cm (1½-inch) fluted mini brioche pans.

6 sheets shortcrust pastry

¼ cup (60ml) brandy

2 teaspoons powdered gelatine

½ cup (125ml) milk

½ tablespoon instant coffee granules

75g (2½ ounces) dark (bittersweet 85%) chocolate

2 egg yolks

¼ cup (55g) caster (superfine) sugar

⅔ cup (160ml) thickened (heavy) cream

125g (4 ounces) raspberries

⅓ cup (35g) dutch cocoa

1 Preheat oven to 180°C/350°F. Grease 24 x 4cm (1½-inch) fluted mini brioche tins.

2 Using the 9cm cutter, cut 24 rounds from pastry sheets. Press pastry rounds into tins; prick bases with a fork. Bake tarts for 10 minutes or until pastry is golden; cool.

3 Place brandy in a small jug, sprinkle over gelatine; place in a small saucepan of simmering water, stir until gelatine dissolves. Cool 5 minutes.

4 Place milk and coffee in a small saucepan; stir, over medium-high heat until coffee dissolves and mixture comes almost to the boil.

5 Melt chocolate (see page 113).

6 Whisk egg yolks and sugar in a medium bowl with an electric mixer until mixture is light and frothy. Gradually whisk in hot coffee mixture. Return mixture to the pan; stir over low heat with a wooden spoon until mixture thickens and coats the back of the spoon (do not boil mixture). Remove pan from heat, whisk in gelatine mixture, then chocolate; cool to room temperature.

7 Meanwhile, whisk cream in a small bowl with an electric mixer until soft peaks form; fold cream into chocolate mixture. Fill pastry cases with mousse; refrigerate for 3 hours or overnight.

8 To serve, top each tartlet with a raspberry; dust with sifted cocoa.

tip Buy a good-quality shortcrust pastry from delis, or make your own.
do-ahead Tarts can be made a day ahead; store, covered, in the fridge.

nutritional count per tartlet
▶ 13.2g total fat
▶ 6.4g saturated fat
▶ 931kJ (222 cal)
▶ 21.8g carbohydrate
▶ 3.4g protein
▶ 1g fibre

trio of orange panna cotta

PREP + COOK TIME 50 MINUTES (+ REFRIGERATION) **MAKES** 24

¾ cup (180ml) milk

6 cups (1.5 litres) thickened (heavy) cream

1½ cups (330g) caster (superfine) sugar

2 tablespoons finely grated orange zest

6 teaspoons powdered gelatine

½ cup (125ml) water

⅔ cup (160ml) strained blood orange juice

⅔ cup (160ml) strained orange juice

orange food colouring

2 tablespoons orange blossom water

1 small blood orange (180g), segmented

1 small orange (180g), segmented

6 small edible flowers, optional (see tips)

1 Place milk, cream, sugar and zest in a medium saucepan. Cook, stirring, over low heat until sugar dissolves and mixture comes almost to the boil; remove from heat.

2 Sprinkle gelatine over the water in a small heatproof jug; stand jug in a small saucepan of simmering water. Stir until gelatine dissolves; cool 5 minutes. Stir gelatine into cream mixture until combined. Divide panna cotta mixture into 3 heatproof jugs.

3 Bring blood orange juice to the boil in a small saucepan; reduce heat to medium, and simmer for 5 minutes or until liquid is reduced to about 2 tablespoons. Cool for 5 minutes, then add to one jug of the panna cotta mixture.

4 Repeat step 3 to reduce the orange juice to about 2 tablespoons. Cool for 5 minutes, then add to the second jug of the panna cotta mixture; tint a pale orange with a couple of drops of food colouring.

5 Stir orange blossom water into the last jug of panna cotta mixture.

6 Rinse 24 x ⅓-cup (80ml) dariole or plastic moulds with cold water – do not dry; place moulds on a tray. Pour each panna cotta mixture into 8 moulds. (You'll have 8 blood orange, 8 orange blossom and 8 orange panna cottas.) Refrigerate panna cottas for 6 hours or overnight.

7 Carefully turn panna cotta out onto a platter (see tip, right). Top blood orange panna cotta with blood orange segments, orange panna cotta with orange segments and the orange blossom panna cotta with edible flowers.

tips We used organic orange blossoms, but you can use any small flower you like. The bold purple of organic violas looks striking against the pale orange panna cotta.
For information on how to segment an orange, see page 113.
do-ahead Panna cotta can be made a day ahead; store, covered, in the fridge.

nutritional count per panna cotta
▶ 23.3g total fat
▶ 14.9g saturated fat
▶ 1199kJ (286 cal)
▶ 17.9g carbohydrate
▶ 2.5g protein
▶ 0.5g fibre

To unmould panna cotta, rub the outside of the mould with a hot kitchen cloth. Holding a mould upside down in your cupped hand, shake gently until the panna cotta releases from the mould; carefully transfer to a serving platter.

COOKING TECHNIQUES

Trimming watercress This peppery green is grown in water; use scissors to cut off the roots then pull the leaves off any thick, woody stems.

Preparing asparagus To snap the woody end off the asparagus, hold it close to the base and bend it until it snaps. Discard the woody end. Trim with a vegetable peeler.

Trimming beetroot Cut the stems to 2cm (¾-inch) of the bulb, and don't trim the beard at the base of the plant. This stops the colour from bleeding during cooking.

To seed a cucumber, cut the cucumber in half lengthways; use a teaspoon to scrape the seeds out into a bowl without piercing the skin.

Washing leeks removes any grit from the inside layers. Cut in half lengthwise, stopping at the root. Fan the layers out and wash under fast-running cold water.

To peel a prawn, hold the body with one hand, twist the head with the other and pull it away from the body. Roll the shell off from the underside with the legs still attached. If you are removing the tail shell, squeeze the tail on both sides to release the shell from the flesh and remove.

Crushing garlic Press unpeeled garlic firmly with the flat blade of a large knife (top) crushing the clove. Pull off the papery skin and chop the clove finely with the knife. A garlic press (bottom) removes and leaves the skin behind while crushing the garlic.

To slice a capsicum, cut the top and bottom off and stand it on one end; using a sharp knife, slice down removing all the flesh. Remove and discard the seeds and membranes, and slice the flesh according to the instructions in the recipe.

To segment an orange, cut off the skin and pith. Cut the orange in half lengthways, and cut out the segments between each membrane.

Zesting citrus fruit A zester has very small, and very sharp, holes that cut the rind (the outermost layer of the fruit) into thin ribbons but leaves the bitter pith behind.

Toasting nuts Whether it's almonds, peanuts, walnuts, or any other nut, toasting them is the same. Stir nuts over a low heat in a dry frying pan until golden brown. Remove the nuts immediately from the pan to stop them from burning.

To seed a vanilla pod, cut it in half lengthwise with a sharp knife. Hold the pod and scrape the seeds out with the edge of a teaspoon.

To melt chocolate, place roughly chopped chocolate into a heatproof bowl over a pan of barely simmering water. The water mustn't touch the base of the bowl. Stir chocolate until smooth, and remove from the pan as soon as it's melted.

Spread the melted chocolate evenly over a cold surface, such as a flat oven tray, a laminated chopping board or, best of all, marble. Stand at room temperature until the chocolate is almost set.

There are many ways of making curls: here, we've used a melon baller – just drag it smoothly and evenly across the surface of the chocolate. Remember, you can always remelt your mistakes. If you don't want to go to the trouble of melting chocolate, just drag a sharp vegetable peeler down the side of a chocolate block to make small curls.

To hull a strawberry The hull, or calyx, is the green leafy top. Cut around the leafy top and into the pale flesh underneath, and discard. Wash and drain the strawberries before using.

GLOSSARY

AMERICAN-STYLE PORK RIBS pork spare ribs that are sold in long slabs or racks of 10 to 12 ribs, trimmed so that little fat remains.

ANGOSTURA BITTERS brand name of a type of aromatic bitters, used mainly in drinks, from aperitifs and cocktails to digestifs, but also desserts and savoury dishes. Its recipe is a closely guarded secret, but it is infused with many herbs and spices.
orange bitters aromatic bitters infused with citrus flavours.

BACON, SHORTCUT is a 'half rasher'; the streaky (belly), narrow portion of the rasher has been removed leaving the choice cut eye meat (fat end).

BAKING POWDER a raising agent consisting mainly of two parts cream of tartar to one part bicarbonate of soda (baking soda).

BAMBOO SHOOTS the tender shoots of bamboo plants, available in cans; must be drained and rinsed before use.

BEANS
broad also known as fava, windsor and horse beans; available dried, fresh, canned and frozen. Fresh and frozen should be peeled twice (discarding both the outer long green pod and the beige-green tough inner shell).
sprouts also known as bean shoots; tender new growths of assorted beans and seeds germinated for consumption. The most readily available are soya bean, mung bean, alfalfa and snow pea sprouts.
white in this book, some recipes may simply call for 'white beans', a generic term we use for canned or dried haricot, cannellini, navy or great northern beans; each can be substituted for the other.

BEEF
fillet steak cut from the tenderloin.
sirloin from the lower portion of the ribs.

BEETROOT also known as red beets or beets; a firm, round root vegetable.

BICARBONATE OF SODA also known as baking or carb soda; a mild alkali used as a leavening agent in baking.

BREAD
afghan a flatbread, similar to lavash or naan breads – can be rectangular or oval in shape; is the national bread of Afghanistan. Baked in a tandoor oven, its texture is dense enough that it is used to pick up foods.
mountain a thin, dry, soft-textured bread that can be filled and rolled up.
panini the word panino is Italian for 'small bread roll'; its plural form is panini. Also the type of a toasted sandwich. Available from supermarkets.
sourdough made from a yeast starter culture used to make the previous loaf of bread. A low-risen bread with a dense centre and crisp crust. May or may not have a sour taste.
tortillas thin, round unleavened bread originating in Mexico. Two kinds are available, one made from wheat flour and the other from corn (maize meal).

BREADCRUMBS
japanese also known as panko; available in two kinds: larger pieces and fine crumbs; have a lighter texture than Western-style breadcrumbs. Available from Asian grocery stores. Unless you make rather coarse breadcrumbs from white bread that's either quite stale or gently toasted, nothing is an adequate substitution. Gives a crunchy texture with a delicate, pale golden colour.
packaged fine-textured, crunchy, purchased white breadcrumbs.
stale one- or two-day-old bread made into crumbs by blending or processing.

BUTTER 125g is equal to one stick (4 ounces) of butter.
unsalted often called 'sweet' butter, simply has no added salt. It is mainly used in baking, and if the recipe calls for unsalted butter, then it should not be substituted.

BUTTERMILK originally the term given to the slightly sour liquid left after butter was churned from cream, today it is commercially made similarly to yogurt. Sold alongside all fresh milk products in supermarkets; despite the implication of its name, it is low in fat.

BUTTERNUT PUMPKIN (squash) a member of the gourd family. Butternut is pear-shaped with a golden skin and orange flesh.

CALAMARI a mollusc, a type of squid.

CAPERS the grey-green buds of a warm climate (usually Mediterranean) shrub, sold either dried and salted or pickled in a vinegar brine. Baby capers, those picked early, are very small, fuller-flavoured and more expensive than the full-sized ones. Capers, whether packed in brine or in salt, must be rinsed well before using.

CHEESE
fetta a crumbly goat- or sheep-milk cheese with a sharp salty taste.
persian fetta is a soft, creamy fetta marinated in a blend of olive oil, garlic, herbs and spices. It is available from most larger supermarkets.
pizza a blend of grated mozzarella, cheddar and parmesan cheeses.

CHICKEN
breast fillet skinned and boned.
tenderloin thin tender strip of meat lying just under the breast.
thigh fillet skin and bone removed.
wing nibbles similar to chicken drumettes. Pre-cut chicken wing and drumstick pieces; if unavailable use chicken drumettes.

CHILLI
jalapeño hot green chillies, available bottled, in brine, or fresh from specialty greengrocers.
red thai also known as 'scuds'; small, very hot and bright red in colour.

CHINESE BARBECUED PORK also called char siew. Traditionally cooked in special ovens, this pork has a sweet-sticky coating made from soy sauce, sherry, five-spice powder and hoisin sauce. Available from Asian food stores.

CHINESE COOKING WINE also known as shao hsing or chinese rice wine. Found in Asian food shops; if you can't find it, replace with mirin or sherry.

CHOCOLATE
dark eating also known as semi-sweet or luxury chocolate; made of a high percentage of cocoa liquor and cocoa butter, and a little added sugar.
Melts discs of compound chocolate ideal for melting and moulding.

CORIANDER a herb that is also available ground or as seeds; do not substitute either of these for fresh, as the tastes are completely different.

CORNFLOUR also known as cornstarch; used as a thickening agent. Available as 100% maize (corn) and wheaten cornflour.

CORNICHON French for gherkin, is a very small variety of pickled cucumber; when pickled with dill they are known as a dill pickle. Available from most major supermarkets and delicatessens.

CREAM we use fresh cream, also known as pouring, single and pure cream; it has no additives. Minimum fat content 35%.

light sour has a fat content of 18.5%.
sour a thick, commercially cultured soured cream. Minimum fat content 35%.
thickened (heavy) a whipping cream containing a thickener. Minimum fat content 35%.

CRÈME FRAÎCHE mature fermented cream having a slightly tangy, nutty flavour and velvety texture. Minimum fat content 35%.

CUSTARD POWDER instant mixture used to make pouring custard; similar to North American instant pudding mixes.

DRIED SHRIMP (goong hang) salted sun-dried prawns ranging in size from not much larger than a rice seed to about 1cm in length. Sold, shelled as a rule, in packages in all Asian grocery stores.

DUTCH COCOA is treated with an alkali to neutralize its acids. It has a reddish-brown colour, mild flavour, and is easy to dissolve in liquids.

EDIBLE GOLD LEAF can be either thin flakes or sheets of gold of very high purity. From specialised cake decorating stores.

ELDERFLOWER CORDIAL an infusion of elderflower flowers and a sugar syrup. Available from some delicatessens. Can be substituted with orange, lemon or lime cordial.

FIRM WHITE FISH FILLET blue eye, bream, flathead, swordfish, ling, whiting, jewfish, snapper or sea perch are all good choices. Check for any small bones and use tweezers to remove them.

FLOUR
00 a fine-grain plain flour, resulting in airy, light bread and soft, delicate pasta.
besan also known as chickpea flour or gram; made from ground chickpeas so is gluten-free and high in protein.
bread a strong flour, meaning it has a relatively high gluten content; good for bread. Available from most supermarkets.
plain an all-purpose flour made from wheat. Not as strong as bread flour.
self-raising (rising) plain or wholemeal flour combined with baking powder in the proportion of 1 cup flour to 2 teaspoons baking powder.

FRIED SHALLOT (homm jiew) is used as a condiment on the table or sprinkled over cooked dishes. Available canned or in cellophane bags at Asian grocery stores; once opened, it will last for ages if stored tightly sealed.

GELATINE we use powdered gelatine. It is also available in sheet form, known as leaf gelatine.

GOW GEE WRAPPERS similar to wonton wrappers, spring roll or egg pastry sheets, all of which can be substituted.

HORSERADISH CREAM creamy paste made of grated horseradish, vinegar, oil and sugar.

INSTANT MASH POTATO MIX dry mashed potato reconstituted with boiling liquid giving a light buttery flavour.

JUNIPER BERRIES the dried fruit from the evergreen tree of the same name, found in specialty spice stores and better delicatessens. Used to flavour gin.

LAMB
backstrap the larger fillet from a row of loin chops or cutlets.
cutlets small, tender rib chop.

MAYONNAISE we use mayonnaise made with whole eggs in our recipes.
japanese made using rice vinegar or apple cider vinegar, along with a small amount of mustard and MSG. It is generally richer in taste than Western-style mayonnaise.

MICRO HERBS harvested as the tiny first leaves emerge.

MIRIN a Japanese champagne-coloured cooking wine; made of glutinous rice and alcohol and used only for cooking. Should not be confused with sake.

MIZUNA Japanese in origin, mizuna is a frizzy green salad leaf with a delicate mustard flavour. Available from greengrocers and supermarkets.

MUSSELS should be bought from a fish market where there is reliably fresh fish. They must be tightly closed when bought, indicating they are alive. Before cooking, scrub the shells with a strong brush and remove the 'beards'. Some mussels might not open, and may need prompting with a knife, or might not have cooked as quickly as the others – you do not have to discard these, just open with a knife and cook a little more if you wish.

MUSTARD
dijon a pale brown, distinctively flavoured, fairly mild french mustard.
english an extremely hot powdered mustard containing ground mustard seeds (both black or brown and yellow-white), wheat flour and turmeric. Also available in a milder, less hot, version.

seeds, black also known as brown mustard seeds; more pungent than the yellow (or white) seeds used in most prepared mustards.
wholegrain also known as seeded. A french-style coarse-grain mustard made from crushed mustard seeds and dijon-style french mustard.

NORI SHEETS a type of dried seaweed used in Japanese cooking as a flavouring, garnish or to make sushi. Sold in thin sheets, plain or toasted (yaki-nori). The thin, dark sheets are usually a dark purplish-black, but they turn green and acquire a pleasant, nutty flavour when toasted. Available from Asian food stores and most supermarkets.

OLIVES, SICILIAN smooth, fine-skinned green olive with a crisp and crunchy texture, and a refreshingly piquant, buttery flavour.

PANCETTA Italian bacon that is cured but not smoked.

PAPRIKA a ground dried sweet red capsicum; many types are available, including sweet, hot, mild and smoked.

PARSLEY
curly has sharp curly leaves and is less flavourful than flat-leaf parsley. It is mainly used as a garnish.
flat-leaf also known as continental parsley or italian parsley.

PEKING DUCK PANCAKES small, round crêpes or pancakes made with plain flour; they can be purchased in Asian food stores. To prepare pancakes, place in a steamer set over a large pan of simmering water. Steam for about 5 minutes or until warm and pliable.

PERSIAN FAIRY FLOSS also sold as Pashmak, is a form of Persian/Iranian fairy floss made from sesame and sugar. It has a different texture and its strands are said to resemble sheep's wool (pashmak in Persian means 'little wool'). It is available from specialist food stores, some delicatessens and cake decorating suppliers.

PIRI PIRI (peri peri) an African word for chilli and also a hot chilli sauce used in Portuguese, African and Brazilian cookery.

POMEGRANATE a dark-red, leathery-skinned fruit about the size of an orange; filled with hundreds of seeds, each wrapped in an edible lucent-crimson pulp having a tangy sweet-sour flavour.

PROSCIUTTO a kind of unsmoked Italian ham; salted, air-cured and aged, it is usually eaten uncooked.

PROSECCO a sparkling Italian wine. Available from selected bottle shops, or substitute with any dry sparkling wine.

RICE PAPER ROUNDS softened in hot water and used as a wrapper for food. Made from ground rice flour, salt and water; sold packaged in either round or square pieces.

ROSEWATER distilled from rose petals, and used in the Middle East, North Africa, and India to flavour desserts. Do not confuse with rose essence, which is more concentrated.

SASHIMI GRADE SEAFOOD raw fish sold as sashimi has to meet stringent guidelines regarding its handling and treatment after leaving the water. Seek advice from local authorities before eating any raw seafood.

SAUCE
barbecue a spicy, tomato-based sauce used to baste or as a condiment.
fish also called nam pla or nuoc nam; made from pulverised salted fermented fish, most often anchovies. Has a pungent smell and strong taste, so use sparingly.
hoisin a thick, sweet and spicy chinese paste made from salted fermented soya beans, onions and garlic.
HP sauce a blend of tomatoes, malt vinegar, molasses, dates, tamarind and spices.
oyster Asian in origin, this rich, brown sauce is made from oysters and their brine, cooked with salt and soy sauce, and thickened with starches.
soy also known as sieu, is made from fermented soya beans. Several variations are available in most supermarkets and Asian food stores.
dark soy is deep brown, almost black in colour; rich, with a thicker consistency than other types. Pungent, though not particularly salty, it is good for marinating.
light soy is a fairly thin, pale but salty tasting sauce; used in dishes in which the natural colour of the ingredients is to be maintained. Do not confuse with salt-reduced or low-sodium soy sauces.
kecap manis is a dark, thick sweet soy sauce used in most South-East Asian cuisines. The soy's sweetness is derived from the addition of either molasses or palm sugar when brewed.

tamari is a thick, dark soy sauce made mainly from soya beans without the wheat used in standard soy sauce.

SHRIMP PASTE often sold as blachan or trasi in Asian food stores; use sparingly because a little goes a long way.

SNOW PEAS also called mange tout ('eat all').

SPICES
baharat is a spice combination from the eastern Mediterranean consisting of chilli, black pepper, paprika, cloves, cinnamon, nutmeg, cardamom, cumin and coriander. Found in Middle-Eastern food stores and specialist spice shops.
dukkah an Egyptian spice blend made with roasted nuts and aromatic spices. It is available from Middle-Eastern food stores, specialty spice stores and some larger supermarkets.
ras el hanout is a classic blend used in Moroccan cooking. The name means 'top of the shop' or the very best spice blend that a spice merchant has to offer. Most versions contain over a dozen spices, including cardamom, nutmeg, mace, cinnamon and ground chilli.
sumac a purple-red, astringent spice ground from berries growing on shrubs around the Mediterranean; it has a tart, lemony flavour.
za'atar a Middle-Eastern blend of roasted dried spices, usually sesame seeds, wild marjoram, thyme and sumac; available in Middle-Eastern food and spice shops and delicatessens.

SUGAR
brown a finely granulated, extremely soft sugar retaining molasses for its characteristic colour and flavour.
caster also known as superfine or finely granulated table sugar.
icing also known as confectioners' sugar or powdered sugar; granulated sugar crushed together with a small amount of cornflour (about 3%).
palm also known as jaggery or gula melaka; made from the sap of the sugar palm tree. Light brown to dark-brown in colour and usually sold in rock-hard cakes; substitute it with brown sugar if unavailable.
white coarsely granulated table sugar, also known as crystal sugar.

TAHINI sesame seed paste; available from Middle-Eastern food stores. Most often used in hummus, baba ghanoush and other Lebanese recipes.

SUSHI RICE a soft, tender short-grain rice. When cooked it is clingy enough to be eaten with chopsticks. If sushi rice is unavailable, substitute with a white short-grain rice such as arborio.

TAMARIND CONCENTRATE (or paste) the distillation of tamarind juice into a condensed, compacted paste. Thick and purple-black, it is ready-to-use with no soaking or straining required; can be diluted with water according to taste.

TEMPURA BATTER MIX an authentic Japanese blend that allows you to create tempura seafood or vegetables quickly and easily at home.

VEAL AND PORK MINCE some butchers sell a pork and veal mixture. If this is not available, buy half the required amount as pork mince and half as veal mince. If the mixture is available buy the total quantity as pork and veal mince.

VIETNAMESE MINT not a mint at all, but a pungent and peppery narrow-leafed member of the buckwheat family. Not confined to Vietnam, it is also known as Cambodian mint, pak pai (Thailand), laksa leaf (Indonesia), daun kesom (Singapore) and rau ram in Vietnam.

VINEGAR
apple cider made from fermented apples.
balsamic white condiment is a clear and lighter version of balsamic vinegar; it has a fresh, sweet clean taste.
red wine based on fermented red wine.
rice wine made from rice wine lees (sediment left after fermentation), salt and alcohol.
white made from spirit of cane sugar.
white wine made from a blend of white wines.

WASABI PASTE an Asian horseradish used to make the pungent, green-coloured sauce traditionally served with Japanese raw fish dishes; also sold in powdered form.

WONTON WRAPPERS also known as wonton skins; made of flour, eggs and water, they come in varying thicknesses. Found in the refrigerated section of supermarkets; gow gee, egg or spring roll pastry sheets can be substituted.

YOGHURT we use plain, unflavoured yoghurt, unless otherwise specified.
greek-style full-cream yoghurt often made from sheep milk; the milk liquids are drained off leaving a thick, smooth consistency with a tart taste.

INDEX

NORFOLK LIBRARY &
INFORMATION SERVICES

7071964

Bertrams   01836106

NML   £6.99

641.568

PARTY FOOD SAVOURY A
Party food : savoury and sweet
796837/00020 - 4 of 5

Published in 2013 by Bauer Media Books
Bauer Media Books is a division of Bauer Media Limited
54 Park St, Sydney
GPO Box 4088, Sydney, NSW 2001.
phone (02) 9282 8618; fax (02) 9126 3702
www.awwcookbooks.com.au

MEDIA GROUP
BAUER MEDIA BOOKS

Publishing Director - Gerry Reynolds
Publisher - Sally Wright
Editorial and Food Director - Pamela Clark
Sales & Rights Director Brian Cearnes
Creative Director - Hieu Chi Nguyen

Published and Distributed in the United Kingdom by Octopus Publishing Group
Endeavour House
189 Shaftesbury Avenue
London WC2H 8JY
United Kingdom
phone (+44)(0)207 632 5400; fax (+44)(0)207 632 5405
info@octopus-publishing.co.uk;
www.octopusbooks.co.uk

Printed by Toppan Printing Co., China

International foreign language rights, Brian Cearnes, Bauer Media Books bcearnes@bauer-media.com.au

A catalogue record for this book is available from the British Library.
ISBN: 978-74245-377-4 (pbk.)
© Bauer Media Ltd 2013
ABN 18 053 273 546

This publication is copyright. No part of it may be reproduced or transmitted
in any form without the written permission of the Publisher.

THE AUSTRALIAN
Women's Weekly

TRIPLE TESTED · FOR YOUR SUCCESS EVERY TIME!

ALSO FROM THE BEST-SELLING COOKERY SERIES OF ALL TIME

THE AUSTRALIAN Women's Weekly **slow cooker**

Delicious winter favourites creamy turkey stew with mustard p50 lamb shank, fennel and vegetable soup p8 borscht p11 pork and fennel soup p16 best-ever bolognese sauce p38 chicken cacciatore p39 coq au vin p44 chinese chicken hot pot p48 osso buco with mixed mushrooms p56 portuguese-style chicken p77 greek-style roast lamb with potatoes p81 red curry lamb shanks p84 mandarin and almond pudding p112

THE AUSTRALIAN Women's Weekly **afternoon tea**

Treat yourself with orange almond victoria sponge p104 neenish & pineapple tarts p37 custard fruit flans p38 cucumber sandwiches p6 vanilla bean scones p17 chocolate éclairs p30 cherry bakewell tarts p42 rhubarb frangipane tarts p46 portuguese custard tarts p50 madeleines p56 chocolate french macaroons p63 rosewater meringues p68 jelly cakes p96 raspberry cream sponge p108 mixed berry hazelnut cake p111

THE AUSTRALIAN Women's Weekly **100 classic cakes**

Some of the recipes in this book: almond butter cake; angel food cake; banana caramel layer cake; carrot cake with lemon cream cheese frosting; celebration fruit cake; chocolate coconut squares; devil's food cake; mississippi mud cake; opera gateau; sacher torte; cinnamon teacake; cut & keep butter cake; featherlight sponge cake

Women's Weekly **the 21-Day Wonder Diet**
21 different daily menus · shopping list · diet diary · advice on healthy eating
Lose up to 10kg in three weeks

THE AUSTRALIAN Women's Weekly **kids' birthday cakes**
MORE THAN 200,000 COPIES SOLD

Happy birthday to you! the magic toadstool p4 whirlipop p7 lazy ladybird p16 this little piggy p24 picture perfect p31 the pirate's dagger p32 the penguin prince p35 party piñata p36 you wacky wabbit p47 friendly flutterby p48 funny faces p52 king of pops p55 rainbow's end p56 lamington choo choo p63 françois ze frog p67 castle of darkness p68 sam the tool man p71 girlie ghost p76 one p92 three p96 seven p104 nine p108
PATTERN SHEET INCLUDED

THE AUSTRALIAN Women's Weekly **Moroccan and the foods of North Africa**
REPRINTED BY POPULAR DEMAND

Get cooking with tomato, olive and radish salad p17 harira p25 butter bean dip p13 beetroot, fennel and lentil salad p14 tuna salad p30 grilled eggplant with tabbouleh p36 fried zucchini p40 roasted pumpkin couscous p44 pumpkin and split pea tagine p48 chicken with couscous stuffing p57 harissa marinated lamb p62 kofta p66 za'atar lamb p70 beef and prune tagine p76 poached nectarines p103 semolina slice p108

Women's Weekly **salad** from classics to contemporary

THE AUSTRALIAN Women's Weekly **jam** jams, jellies & pickles

Women's Weekly **cool cupcakes**

Women's Weekly **pie** fresh from the oven

To order books visit www.octopusbooks.co.uk or telephone 01903 828 503